921
COL

Plantz, Connie.

Bessie Coleman.

$20.95

34880030011428

DATE			

BESSIE
COLEMAN

The African-American Biographies Series

MARIAN ANDERSON
Singer and Humanitarian
0-7660-1211-5

MAYA ANGELOU
More Than a Poet
0-89490-684-4

LOUIS ARMSTRONG
King of Jazz
0-89490-997-5

ARTHUR ASHE
Breaking the Color Barrier
in Tennis
0-89490-689-5

BENJAMIN BANNEKER
Astronomer and Mathematician
0-7660-1208-5

JULIAN BOND
Civil Rights Activist and Chairman of the NAACP
0-7660-1549-1

RALPH BUNCHE
Winner of the Nobel Peace Prize
0-7660-1203-4

BESSIE COLEMAN
First Black Woman Pilot
0-7660-1545-9

W. E. B. DU BOIS
Champion of Civil Rights
0-7660-1209-3

PAUL LAURENCE DUNBAR
Portrait of a Poet
0-7660-1350-2

DUKE ELLINGTON
Giant of Jazz
0-89490-691-7

ARETHA FRANKLIN
Motown Superstar
0-89490-686-0

NIKKI GIOVANNI
Poet of the People
0-7660-1238-7

WHOOPI GOLDBERG
Comedian and Movie Star
0-7660-1205-0

LORRAINE HANSBERRY
Playwright and Voice of Justice
0-89490-945-2

MATTHEW HENSON
Co-Discoverer of the North Pole
0-7660-1546-7

LANGSTON HUGHES
Poet of the Harlem Renaissance
0-89490-815-4

ZORA NEALE HURSTON
Southern Storyteller
0-89490-685-2

JESSE JACKSON
Civil Rights Activist
0-7660-1390-1

QUINCY JONES
Musician, Composer, Producer
0-89490-814-6

BARBARA JORDAN
Congresswoman, Lawyer,
Educator
0-89490-692-5

CORETTA SCOTT KING
Striving for Civil Rights
0-89490-811-1

MARTIN LUTHER KING, JR.
Leader for Civil Rights
0-89490-687-9

KWEISI MFUME
Congressman and NAACP Leader
0-7660-1237-9

TONI MORRISON
Nobel Prize-Winning Author
0-89490-688-7

WALTER DEAN MYERS
Writer for Real Teens
0-7660-1206-9

JESSE OWENS
Track and Field Legend
0-89490-812-X

COLIN POWELL
Soldier and Patriot
0-89490-810-3

A. PHILIP RANDOLPH
Union Leader and Civil Rights Crusader
0-7660-1544-0

PAUL ROBESON
Actor, Singer, Political Activist
0-89490-944-4

JACKIE ROBINSON
Baseball's Civil Rights Legend
0-89490-690-9

BETTY SHABAZZ
Sharing the Vision
of Malcolm X
0-7660-1210-7

HARRIET TUBMAN
Moses of the Underground Railroad
0-7660-1548-3

MADAM C. J. WALKER
Self-Made Businesswoman
0-7660-1204-2

IDA B. WELLS-BARNETT
Crusader Against Lynching
0-89490-947-9

OPRAH WINFREY
Talk Show Legend
0-7660-1207-7

CARTER G. WOODSON
Father of African-American History
0-89490-946-0

—African-American Biographies—

BESSIE COLEMAN

First Black Woman Pilot

Series Consultant:
Dr. Russell L. Adams, Chairman
Department of Afro-American Studies, Howard University

Connie Plantz

Enslow Publishers, Inc.

40 Industrial Road   PO Box 38
Box 398   Aldershot
Berkeley Heights, NJ 07922   Hants GU12 6BP
USA   UK
http://www.enslow.com

To Dad, who taught me about airplanes,
and Mom, who gave me a love of reading.

Library of Congress Cataloging-in-Publication Data

Plantz, Connie.
    Bessie Coleman : first black woman pilot / by Connie Plantz.
        p. cm. (African-American Biographies)
    Includes bibliographical references and index.
    ISBN 0-7660-1545-9
    1. Coleman, Bessie, 1892–1926—Juvenile literature. 2. Women air
pilots—United States—Juvenile literature. [1. Coleman, Bessie,
1892–1926. 2. Air pilots. 3. African Americans—Biography.
4. Women—Biography.] I. Title. 2. Series
TL540.C646 P58 2001
629.13'092-dc21
    [B]   00-012424
                                                      CIP
                                                       AC

Printed in the United States of America

10 9 8 7 6 5 4 3 2

To Our Readers: We have done our best to make sure all Internet addresses in this book
were active and appropriate when we went to press. However, the author and the publisher
have no control over and assume no liability for the material available on those Internet sites
or on other Web sites they may link to. Any comments or suggestions can be sent by e-mail
to comments@enslow.com or to the address on the back cover.

Every effort has been made to locate all copyright holders of material used in this book. If
any errors or omissions have occurred, corrections will be made in future editions of this
book.

Illustration Credits: © Corel Corporation, p. 51; Brandon Plantz, pp. 100, 105; The Black
Film Center/Archive and the Lilly Library, Indiana University, Bloomington Indiana, p. 83;
Chicago Defender, pp. 64, 74; Courtesy of the Florida State Archives, pp. 71, 94; Courtesy of
the Steamship Historical Society of America, p. 44; Courtesy Ellis County Museum, pp. 15,
23, 26; From the Eartha M. M. White Collection, Thomas G. Carpenter Library, University
of North Florida, p. 91; Jean Byrd, p. 18; The Miriam Matthews Collection, California
African-American Museum, p. 11; National Air and Space Museum, Smithsonian Institution
(SI Neg. No. 80-12873, p. 6 ; SI Neg. No. 88-7993, p. 30; SI Neg. No. 93-7758, p. 49; SI
Neg. No. 84-14782, p. 58 ; SI Neg. No. 85-7754, p. 60); Photographs and Prints Division,
Schomburg Center for Research in Black Culture, The New York Public Library, Astor,
Lenox and Tilden Foundations, pp. 33, 41, 85; Richard A. Chapman/Reprinted with special
permission from the *Chicago Sun-Times*, Inc. © 2001, p. 109; San Diego Aerospace Museum
Library and Archives, pp. 9, 35, 47.

Cover Credit: National Air and Space Museum, Smithsonian Institution
(SI Neg. No. 80-12873).

CONTENTS

Bessie Coleman

1

FLYING WITH A PURPOSE

Flying at sixty miles an hour in a borrowed biplane, Bessie Coleman gradually slowed her speed. The plane began to dive. Dangerously close to the earth, she pulled the throttle in to give the engine more power. Then, effortlessly, she flew back toward the clouds. It was June 19, 1925. Thousands of spectators at the old speedway auto racetrack in Houston, Texas, cheered and stomped their feet.

Pilot Lincoln Beachey had complained in 1913, "I am convinced that the only thing that draws crowds to see me is the morbid desire to see something happen.

They call me the Master Birdman, but they pay to see me die."[1] In 1925 nothing had changed. Newspapers were full of black-and-white pictures of crumpled crashed planes. Undertakers chased Hubert Julian, an African-American daredevil pilot who desired fame so much that he performed stunts no one else would try. His outlandish maneuvers caused the morticians to believe he would soon crash. They went to his shows and begged him for the rights to display his body after he died. Later, unemployed World War I pilots bought used planes to dazzle audiences with outrageous routines that appeared life-threatening. Amateur stunt performers danced the Charleston on the upper wings of biplanes or dangled from rope ladders.

These stunt pilots went from one county fair to the next, entertaining crowds with their dangerous maneuvers. Some people called them "barnstormers." This was a term used for traveling performers who brought their shows to rural areas. Others called the aviators "flying fools" because of their recklessness. A 1921 *New York Times* editorial illustrated the absurdity of these daredevil tricks. It stated that so many pilots had died in crashes that no one cared anymore. Only their relatives and friends showed any emotion when reports of pilots' deaths were printed in the newspaper.[2]

Bessie Coleman was far from being a flying fool. She was an African-American woman with a goal. An article in the *Houston Post-Dispatch* on June 18, 1925,

The daring pilots who entertained crowds with their death-defying stunts were known as barnstormers.

reported that Coleman was attracting attention all over the country for her efforts to interest African Americans in aviation.[3] Her goal, she told them, was to get African Americans flying. Coleman stressed that African Americans were the only group of people in the world who had not been involved in aviation. The *Houston Post-Dispatch* was written and read by whites. Usually, Coleman's exhibitions were covered only in newspapers read by blacks. The fact that this paper reported Coleman's achievements indicated that she had become an entertainer of interest to all audiences.

Bessie Coleman chose June 19 for this exhibition of flying because it was an important date in African-American history: Sixty years earlier, on June 19, 1865, Union troops came to Galveston, Texas, and announced the end of the Civil War. The slaves there learned that they were all free. Coleman, herself a native Texan, used the annual celebration, called Juneteenth, to interest her people in aviation. Every loop-the-loop, barrel roll, and figure eight showed the audience on the ground that an African American could fly a plane. As Bessie Coleman zipped through the sky, her message was as clear as skywriting: Don't be afraid to take risks. Fly!

As she prepared for her last stunt of the show, Coleman checked the windsock attached to a fence post. Seeing the white fabric blowing westward, she knew the wind was coming from the east. Coleman turned her plane to face into the wind. Then, to give the audience one more thrill, she stopped her loud buzzing engine. In complete silence, she glided the plane to the ground. The forward motion dragged the plane's tail across the rough field. A brass band played a jazzy tune as Coleman coasted to a stop. It was a perfect landing.

Coleman whipped off her goggles and loosened her leather helmet strap. She climbed out of the cockpit onto the lower wing, then jumped to the ground. Her petite figure was fashionably dressed in a tailored flying suit and a leather French officer's jacket. Coleman confidently smiled and waved at the crowd.

The spectators whistled and hooted. They pushed onto the field toward five planes waiting to give them rides. About seventy-five people, mostly women, lined up. They were eager for a turn to climb aboard for a bird's-eye view of Houston.

Coleman wanted to interest other African Americans in flying.

The pilots had two problems. First, they didn't have enough planes to carry everyone who wanted to go. Second, they could not fly as fast as the passengers wanted. But despite these problems, the *Houston Informer*, a black newspaper, called this historical event "the biggest thrill of the evening—and of a lifetime, for that matter." It was the first time African Americans in the South had been given the opportunity to fly.[4]

On June 19, 1925, Bessie Coleman accomplished her goal. She demonstrated that an African American could pilot an airplane.

2

GROWING UP SOUTHERN

n January 26, 1892, Bessie Coleman was born to Susan and George Coleman. The Colemans were both African American. George was also part Choctaw Indian.[1] With Bessie's birth, there were now six children living in the family's one-room cabin. The Colemans lived on a dirt road in Atlanta, Texas.

Susan Coleman wanted her daughter to grow up experiencing lots of opportunities. But she knew Bessie would have an uphill struggle. The year before Bessie's birth, one hundred African Americans in the United States had died by lynching, murdered by lawless mobs.[2] Women faced discrimination, too. They were not allowed to vote and were considered second-class citizens. Society expected women to stay home to cook, clean, and care for children.

Bessie's older brother John kept her safe, clean, and out of mischief.[3] Every night after Susan Coleman lit the oil lamp, Bessie climbed onto her brother's lap to listen to him read passages from the Bible. Bessie was the baby of the family for two years. Then another daughter, Elois, was born.

On October 15, 1894, George Coleman bought property in Waxahachie, Texas. According to the town records, he spent his savings on "one quarter of an acre, more or less," on Mustang Creek. He paid $25 for this property.[4]

The Colemans moved from the small town of Atlanta to Waxahachie. This city sat in the middle of Ellis County, the largest cotton-producing county in the nation. Cotton yards, cotton warehouses, and cotton mills hummed with activity. The Colemans were not the only newcomers. As the county's cotton production increased—from 389 bales of cotton in 1860 to 106,384 bales in 1910—so did its population. Almost three thousand people moved into Ellis County from 1880 to 1900 to work.[5]

Every day, trains from the New Orleans and the Missouri-Kansas-Texas railroads chugged through the center of town past the flowering crape myrtle trees.

Their whistles signaled hope for Waxahachie residents. The town's residents called their cargo "white oil." Growing a good crop of cotton and selling it was almost as great as discovering oil on your land. Either of these resources could make a farmer rich.

Many of the workers who supported the booming economy of Waxahachie were African American and lived four miles east of the railroad tracks.[6] The Coleman property on Palmer Road was in this African-American section. It had a willow tree and several fruit trees. George Coleman built a three-room shotgun

Bessie was three years old when her family moved to Waxahachie, Texas. Wagons filled with bales of cotton crowded the streets.

house. This type of house is rectangular, with rooms lined up from front to back. It was said that a bullet shot through the front door of such a house could travel straight through all the doorways and exit out the back door.

After Bessie and her family moved into their new home, Susan Coleman planted yellow roses beside the porch and a garden of sweet corn and peanuts in the back. Although they lived a few miles outside the town limits, the Colemans spent a lot of time in the small town.[7]

Susan Coleman made sure her family attended church every Sunday. Inside the African-American Baptist Church, the congregation sang hymns of strength such as "Onward Christian Soldiers" and "Jesus, Savior, Pilot Me." Young and old publicly professed their faith in God. Back at home, the Colemans continued this fellowship by chatting and sharing stories with neighbors.[8]

As Susan Coleman's lilac bushes and sweet-smelling honeysuckle vines grew, so did her family. Mrs. Coleman gave birth to Nilus in 1896, then Georgia in 1898. During Susan's twenty-three years of marriage to George, she had thirteen children. Four of the children died, though there is no record of what caused their deaths. During this time, many African-American babies did not live past infancy. An African-American doctor suggested the cause to be the excessive physical labor performed by pregnant African-American women.[9]

Work never stopped in the Coleman family. When they got older, the three eldest children moved to big cities to find jobs less strenuous than working in the cotton fields. Bessie's brothers John, who was eleven, and Isaiah, fifteen, took their places in the fields. Cotton harvesting meant extra money for the family. It also caused extra housework and baby-sitting for Bessie and Elois. Bessie ground corn for cornmeal, bathed the children, weeded the garden, gathered eggs, and scrubbed the family laundry. Entire days were spent making soap from ashes and lard, and helping with hog butchering. In season, Bessie picked apples, pears, peaches, and plums from the trees on the lower end of the lot.[10]

Susan Coleman always insisted that her children attend school. At age six, Bessie trudged four miles to the one-room African-American school on Aiken Street. Her sister Elois later described the school as well built with good, but not great, teachers. Their strength, she said, was that they tried to make the students feel good about themselves and that they established a feeling of black pride. Especially proud, said Elois, were the parents who could not read or write themselves but watched their children learn these skills. Susan Coleman was one of these parents. Once her daughter Bessie learned to read, it was hard

The Colemans built a small home in this style, with the rooms and doorways all lined up. This type of building was nicknamed "shotgun house" because it was said that a bullet could enter the front door and exit out the back without piercing any walls.

to get her to stop. Reading was her favorite pastime, more fun than playing dolls with her sisters.[11]

Bessie's school was just for African Americans because during this time all aspects of life in the South were segregated. Whites and blacks lived in separate areas, and they were not allowed to attend school together. Laws known as Jim Crow laws restricted where African Americans could go to school, eat, drink, sleep, and even sit. "Whites Only" signs were posted in public places on everything from rest rooms and movie theater entrances to water fountains.

George Coleman resented these laws that limited his rights and freedoms. One day he talked with his wife about moving their family to Indian Territory, now the state of Oklahoma. If they moved there, he said, they would be treated as equals by the Choctaw Indians because of his heritage. When Susan Coleman refused, George went alone. Susan Coleman said, "You can go if you want to, but I am neither a pioneer or squaw." She considered her husband lazy and did not mind his leaving.[12]

Soon after Bessie's father left, her brother Isaiah went to Canada and John moved in with another brother, Walter, who lived in Chicago. Susan Coleman began working as a day cook and housekeeper for Mr. and Mrs. Elwin Jones, a kindly white couple. To help Susan feed the family, Mrs. Jones often gave her a flour sack full of biscuits and cooked steaks.[13] The Joneses owned a plant nursery, and they also gave Susan potted plants to decorate the porch of her small home. Giving food and other items to their workers was a common practice among white employers. Wages were very low, and without this charity, called "pan toting" or "service pan," the families of African-American housekeepers, cooks, and laundresses might have starved.

Susan Coleman turned her work for the Joneses into a learning experience. She watched their table manners, then taught them to her own girls. She made her daughters sit at a cloth-covered table and practice using polite phrases like "please, thank you, and excuse me." They also learned when to use the correct fork and spoon.[14]

Susan Coleman got books for Bessie from a library wagon that passed by the house once or twice a year. Bessie read biographies and poems about strong, proud African Americans. She learned about Booker T. Washington, the former slave who became a famous educator and powerful leader of his people. She read about Harriet Tubman, a runaway slave who helped hundreds of other slaves escape to freedom. She recited poems by African-American poet Paul Laurence Dunbar. One of his best-known poems is "Ode to Ethiopia," which begins, "Be proud, my race, in mind and soul." Another is "Sympathy," with its famous line "I know why the caged bird sings."[15] Dunbar's poetry had been printed in Orville Wright's newspaper, *The Dayton Tattler*, in 1889.

Bessie also read *Uncle Tom's Cabin* by Harriet Beecher Stowe. This book describes the terrible treatment of African-American slaves in the South. The emotional novel caused many to rally against slavery in the time leading up to the Civil War. Bessie's sister Elois later said that when reading this story to the family, Bessie "would brush away a tear, and at times with the sense of humor that she always had, she would laugh, though reluctantly."[16] After reading *Uncle Tom's Cabin*, Bessie vowed never to be like Topsy or Uncle Tom, two of the characters in the story who suffered because of the cruelty of slavery.

As a young girl, Bessie had no choice but to accept her life and all it entailed. Cotton picking was one job she hated, but it was necessary for her and her sisters to help earn money for the family.[17] Every year the cotton season disrupted Bessie's education. Because so many parents needed their children to work in the fields, schools closed from August to December for the harvest.

The planting, chopping, and picking of cotton was strenuous work. To plant, Bessie followed a mule-drawn plow in the hot sun. After dropping seeds onto the tilled soil, she then packed them in with her hands. Once the plants began to grow, Bessie dressed in a long-sleeved blouse to protect her arms from scratches as she thinned out the bushes. Using a hoe, she dug out weeds and grass. Then, when the cotton plants were mature, she spent long hours picking the cotton balls and stuffing them into her sack. One day, instead of helping pick, Bessie was discovered riding on another picker's sack as it dragged along the ground.[18]

Bessie may not have liked working in the fields, but she was extremely helpful at the scales. Every day when her family lined up to weigh the cotton, Bessie noted the pounds of cotton her family picked and the price they were paid per pound. Then she recorded the amounts on paper.[19] Her mathematical skills kept her mother from being cheated by the white overseer.

When the Ringling Brothers Circus rolled into Waxahachie on Wednesday, October 29, 1902, Bessie and Elois were allowed to abandon the fields and rush into town. There, banners hanging from brick buildings promised the appearance of the last giraffe in the world and forty clowns.[20] Lions rolled by in ornately painted wagons pulled by prancing stallions. Elephants swung their trunks to bouncy calliope music. Bessie and Elois each had a half-dollar coin to spend. They brought their own lunch in a pail and saved their money for pink lemonade, popcorn, and balloons.[21]

A year later, eleven-year-old Bessie displayed a knack for selling. She sold the most tickets for the church bazaar and won a harmonica.[22] As a preteen, Bessie also absorbed her mother's strong religious convictions. At age twelve, she was baptized by the minister of the Missionary Baptist Church.

Bessie finished all eight grades at the local school. Then, with her mother's encouragement, she made plans to continue her education. Susan Coleman wanted her daughter to attend the university in Langston, Oklahoma, but they had no money for the

Young Bessie and her sister Elois were thrilled when the Ringling Brothers Circus came to town in 1902.

tuition. Bessie and her mother agreed that Bessie should work as a laundress to earn the money.

Bessie earned only $4 to $8 a month for this hot and heavy work. Each Monday, she crossed the railroad tracks to collect dirty clothes from white families. She would knock on the back doors of their spacious houses—gingerbread-style homes decorated with lacy woodwork ornamentation. Then Bessie carried the laundry to her simple wooden home. On Saturdays, she returned the loads of clean, ironed clothes. If a customer complained of bad soap or a lost sock, Bessie would not be paid.

In 1910, eighteen-year-old Bessie became a student at the Colored Agricultural and Normal University in Langston, Oklahoma. She registered as "Elizabeth Coleman."[23] Besides offering college courses, the university had a preparatory school for new students who did not meet the entrance requirements. Bessie Coleman had missed so much school while picking cotton that she was placed in the sixth grade of the preparatory school.[24]

After one term, Coleman ran out of money and had to return home. She managed to make a big impression as she arrived in Waxahachie: She had persuaded some members of the Langston school band to accompany her on the trip. When friends from Waxahachie's Missionary Baptist Church arrived to greet Coleman's train, she marched onto the platform in style. The lively music of the Langston band transformed her return into a memorable occasion.[25]

Even though Coleman was no longer in school, she was interested in learning, and her mind was always active. Sometimes, at two or three o'clock in the morning, she would wake her sister Elois to tell her that they needed to spend more time just thinking. Then Bessie would suggest a subject, and the two of them would discuss it.[26]

Airplanes were a controversial news item of the time. Newspaper articles told about the "dangerous toys" that flew at unnecessary and perilous speeds of sixty miles an hour. They blamed crashes on mysterious "sky holes." Reporters fussed about unruly, sensation-loving mobs rushing to these crashes. Shouldn't thirty-five or forty miles an hour be fast enough for an airplane? reporters asked. The press featured the wild antics of Lincoln Beachey, the "father of aerobatics." At the San Francisco Exposition, he flew inside a building and smashed himself and the plane into a wall. A few weeks later, he flew into the mist at Niagara Falls, maneuvered his plane under the bridge, and emerged on the Canadian shore. Beachey explained to inventor Thomas A. Edison, who saw his performance, that he set out to do what others thought impossible by combining thought and action.[27]

While the world was changing, Bessie Coleman resumed the dreary work of a laundress. She carried water from the well, boiled the clothes in a pot, then scrubbed them clean on a washboard with homemade lye soap. After rinsing, starching, and wringing them out by hand, she hung the garments out to dry on a rope stretched between two trees. Then, with a heavy iron heated on the top of the stove, Coleman pressed out the wrinkles.

Along with aviation news, newspapers carried daily stories about Chicago, Illinois. Opportunities for a good life, the paper promised, were plentiful in Chicago, where Jim Crow laws were nonexistent. Bessie's brothers John and Walter lived there. They had found jobs that did not involve hard physical labor like doing laundry or picking cotton.

In 1915, twenty-three-year-old Bessie Coleman followed her brothers' example. She left the small town of Waxahachie, Texas, in search of a better life in Chicago, the second-largest city in America.

To earn money, Bessie washed clothes for white families in Waxahachie. Each week, she knocked on the back doors of their big, fancy homes to collect her work.

3

SEEKING
INDEPENDENCE

oleman bought a ticket from the clerk at the
station in Waxahachie. Then she boarded
the crowded train car for black passengers
and squeezed onto a wooden bench.

Coleman arrived in Chicago twenty-four hours
later greeted by the music of Chicago's South Side:
Electric cable cars jiggled beside Model T Fords; trol-
leys rattled past horse-drawn carriages; and elevated
trains zipped by on their way to the Loop, Chicago's
business district. North of the station were magnificent
buildings designed by the world's most imaginative
engineers and architects.[1]

Bessie's brother Walter lived in an area called the Black Belt. It was close to the Union Stockyards, where cattle were penned and slaughtered. Walter Coleman was a quiet and gentle man who had been living in Chicago for ten years. He was married to a woman named Willie. John Coleman and his wife, Elizabeth, were already living in Walter's three-room apartment when Bessie moved in.

Thirty-five-year-old Walter Coleman supported his relatives by working as a Pullman porter on trains running to and from Chicago. Pullman porters earned good wages and were respected by the African-American community. But it was hard, frustrating work. Walter Coleman spent long hours pleasing rude and demanding white train passengers and bosses. He was required to obey the rules posted by the Pullman Company president. One of the rules posted in the porters' sleeping car forbade African-American porters to use the fresh white sheets provided for the white passengers. Instead, the porters had to sleep on old sheets dyed blue. This way white passengers knew they were not sharing sheets with African Americans.[2]

Although Bessie Coleman had a place to live, she needed a job. She immediately began searching. Men's jobs were plentiful in the slaughterhouses or as replacements for striking white workers. But the only jobs available for a woman were scrubbing laundry, mopping floors, or polishing train engines for $3 a day.

Coleman did not take any of these jobs. Instead, she enrolled in the Burnham School of Beauty Culture. New methods for straightening hair and bleaching African-American women's skin were taught at the school. Courses were given on manicuring nails and other beauty treatments and techniques. Coleman enrolled in manicure classes and won a contest for being the best and fastest. She sent her sister Elois a clipping from the *Chicago Defender*, featuring herself as the winning manicurist.[3]

After she graduated from beauty school, Coleman got her first job as a manicurist. She was hired by William Buckner, a trainer for the Chicago White Sox baseball team and owner of the White Sox Barbershop. The barbershop's customers included racketeers, entertainers, and businessmen. While having their nails and hair trimmed, these men made business deals.

Coleman's table stood in the front window of this shop on Thirty-fifth and State Street.[4] From there, she could view the busy activity of the South Side business district. On this street, known as "the Stroll" or "Black Wall Street," dynamic African-American businessmen such as Jesse Binga, owner of the Binga bank, or Robert Abbott, founder of the *Chicago Defender* newspaper, stood on street corners smoking cigars and

Coleman moved to Chicago, where she enrolled in beauty school.
Then she got a job manicuring nails.

talking with friends outside the *Defender*'s headquarters.[5]

At night, jazz permeated the Stroll. Chicago sparkled after dark with lights, snazzily dressed couples, and loud music from the Dreamland and the Royal Gardens. Famous entertainers of the time such as Bill "Bojangles" Robinson often partied on the Stroll until the nightclubs closed. Then they would move on to parties where jazz performers played until dawn in private homes. These were called "house rent parties" because admission fees were charged to help the occupants pay their landlords.[6]

During this time, Walter Coleman introduced Bessie to Claude Glenn. He was a pleasant, quiet man fourteen years older than Bessie. Years later, it was discovered that twenty-four-year-old Bessie Coleman secretly married thirty-eight-year-old Claude Glenn. He applied for a marriage license on December 30, 1916, and they were married on January 30, 1917, in a house ceremony with no relatives present.[7]

Soon after the marriage, Coleman moved from her brother Walter's apartment to her own apartment at 3935 Forest Avenue, but Claude Glenn never lived there with her. Instead, Susan Coleman and Bessie's sisters Georgia, Elois, and Nilus and their six children moved in with her at various times while they were looking for their own places.

Coleman's relatives were not the only southerners

to move to Chicago. Half a million other African Americans arrived during a two-year period. The *Chicago Defender* played a big part in what was known as the Great Northern Drive. Robert Abbott, owner of the newspaper, openly and defiantly encouraged southern African Americans to move to the northern cities for jobs and respect. Not wanting their black laborers to leave, some southern white communities even passed laws prohibiting African Americans from purchasing or reading the *Chicago Defender*. Those caught with the newspaper could be whipped or sent to a prison camp.

But traveling African Americans such as porters, entertainers, and preachers circulated the paper from the North to the South. Abbott did not trust the United States mail carriers in the Deep South to deliver his newspaper. Instead, the *Chicago Defender* was smuggled to half a million customers in barbershops, poolrooms, drugstores, churches, and private homes.

Another reason for the influx of people to Chicago was that northern factories sent agents to the South to entice African-American men north. They knew that blacks would work for lower wages than white workers. Because boll weevils had ruined the cotton crops, unemployed southerners jumped at the chance to work in the city.

Chicago experienced a rise of prejudice as these

new African Americans arrived. Chicago, the promised land, became less promising. Many of the uneducated newcomers failed to find work. Restaurants began to refuse service to African Americans. Blacks were excluded from white residential areas, and ghettos began to form. Violence erupted against African Americans, and many were beaten or stoned by white gangs. African Americans' houses were destroyed with homemade bombs.[8]

The *Chicago Defender*, published from this building, was an important newspaper for African Americans.

Amid these racial tensions, the United States declared war on Germany on April 6, 1917. France and Germany had been fighting since 1914. America wanted to help France win the war. Bessie Coleman's brothers Walter and John joined the all-black 8th Infantry Regiment of the Illinois National Guard.

Flying machines were used in World War I for the first time. The United States did not manufacture the planes used in this war, but on the home front, stories of planes' capabilities spread. These planes were flown by white pilots.

Articles and photographs of the first and second African-American regiments shipped to France made page one of the *Chicago Defender* and the *Chicago Whip*. Bessie Coleman began to think and wonder about the place of African Americans in aviation. Why didn't African Americans fly planes?[9]

The uses for planes were expanding. The United States Post Office Department started delivering mail by plane. On May 15, 1918, President Woodrow Wilson was invited to witness the first airmail flight to take off from Washington, D.C. The president added his own letter to one of the mailbags; it was addressed to the postmaster in New York City. Unfortunately, the pilot's compass was highly inaccurate. He flew off in the wrong direction and crashed in a farmer's field about twenty miles away. The plane flipped over, but the pilot was unhurt.[10]

Flying machines like this "Goliath" bomber were used in World War I for the first time.

Women, too, began to test their flying skills. Katherine Stinson, the fourth licensed woman pilot in the United States, bragged that she could do multiple loops in her biplane. She claimed that this would put women ahead of men in the science of aviation.[11] Newsreels showed her tours in England, China, and Japan. Another prominent woman aviator, Ruth Law, flew a nonstop 590-mile flight from Chicago to New York. She received praise from Admiral Robert Peary, one of the first explorers of the North Pole, who said, "The whole world may now read what a woman can do."[12] Then Stinson beat Law's record by flying 610 miles nonstop.

World War I ended on November 11, 1918. The 8th Infantry Regiment of the Illinois National Guard marched down Michigan Avenue in Chicago. These members of the 370th Infantry had won twenty-one U.S. Distinguished Service Crosses and sixty-eight French War Crosses. The heroic deeds of the African-American soldiers stimulated pride among Chicago's South Side citizens.

The entire Black Belt wrapped itself in patriotism. Bessie Coleman hung a toy plane in the window of the White Sox Barbershop.[13] Smoke shops and men's clothing stores made window displays of war photographs and personal items from the African-American men who had fought in France.

Ironically, after helping to win the battle for democracy, the African-American soldiers returned home to the same bigoted America. More than twenty race riots occurred that summer throughout the United States. The hot summer of 1919 was named "Red Summer" because of all the blood that was shed in racial violence.

Coleman and her family were right in the middle of one riot. The Chicago Race Riot started on Sunday, July 27, after a black youth on a homemade raft drifted into the "white only" part of Lake Michigan. Some white swimmers threw stones, and the young man drowned. Instead of arresting the stone throwers, the police arrested an African American. Angry

African Americans gathered, and one shot at the police. The police returned the fire.

The following day, fighting broke out on the crowded streetcars. Thirty African Americans were injured. Throughout the night, whites entered blacks' homes, dragged the families outside, and whipped them. Young white hoodlums in cars sped through the black area shooting randomly. The governor called in the state militia, and Bessie Coleman's neighborhood was besieged by five thousand poorly trained National Guardsmen. This riot left 38 dead, 537 injured, and more than 1,000 people homeless.[14]

To make matters worse, crime related to illegal liquor sales was on the rise. Congress in 1919 passed the Eighteenth Amendment, which prohibited the drinking and selling of liquor in the United States. Chicago's criminals, seeing an opportunity to make money, began fermenting liquor in basements. Gangster wars erupted over territories for selling the illegal liquor. Different groups of bootleggers tried to dominate various areas of the city through brutality and violence. They hired unemployed, uneducated African-American men to work for them.

Bessie Coleman's brother John got a job with one of these bootleggers. The notorious gangster Alphonse "Scarface" Capone hired John as a cook.[15] Capone's machine-gun tactics terrorized Chicago, but he also had a kind side. He provided needy African Americans with free meals and housing. Black nightclub performers were given jobs and large tips by Capone.[16]

One day John Coleman strutted into the White Sox Barbershop and began teasing Bessie. He started comparing African-American women to French women he had seen during the war. John said that African-American women could not measure up to French women. The French women had careers. They even flew airplanes. He doubted that African-American women could fly like the French women. Bessie waited for the barbershop customers to stop laughing. Then she replied, "That's it. You just called it for me."[17]

4

PASSING THE TEST

essie Coleman sent letters to flight schools in the Chicago area to find out about tuition costs. Each school refused to consider her because she was African American and a woman. The schools admitted only white students.

The majority of the schools in the United States were run by white men who believed that women should not fly. Glenn Curtiss, a plane manufacturer and aviation school owner, thought women belonged on the ground. He feared that "any accident involving a woman pilot would set aviation back for years."[1] (In later years, he did accept women in his school in order to make money.) Orville Wright also rejected female applicants to his school. He believed they were seeking only fame and did not care about learning to fly.[2] When aviator Margery Brown interviewed men about their opinions on women pilots, she received many negative responses. The men said that women made poor pilots because "(1) they are too emotional, (2) they would blow up in a crisis, (3) airplanes are mere playthings to them."[3] One pilot thought that only 10 percent of women had enough intelligence to learn how to fly.

Determined, Bessie Coleman went to the *Chicago Defender* headquarters to see Robert Abbott, the owner of the newspaper. Abbott, a son of former slaves, was an attorney. He was also one of the first African-American millionaires. He encouraged African Americans to talk to him about their worries and concerns. Coleman told Abbott about her plans and ambitions to fly a plane. She asked him for advice about how she could obtain a license. Abbott told Coleman how she could "turn her disadvantages into advantages."[4] He, too, planned to turn her situation into an advantage. Being a businessman, Abbott saw Coleman's ambition as a great promotional opportunity for himself. If Coleman were to become the first African-American woman pilot, the *Chicago Defender* could sponsor her. Reports on Coleman's progress could increase the paper's readership.[5]

"I refused to take no for an answer," said Coleman, who dreamed of learning how to fly a plane. She asked Robert Abbott, owner of the *Chicago Defender*, for advice.

Abbott advised Coleman to go to France to attend an aviation school. In France, he said, she would not face the racism found in the United States. Of course, first she would need to study French.[6] Going to aviation school in France was not an unique idea. France and America were competitors in aviation.

Bessie Coleman's family was opposed to her flying. Coleman said she understood their fears and that she would do everything possible to keep safe. When they worried about the difficulties and risks she would face, she said that if by taking risks she could achieve her dream, then she would never regret trying.[7]

To go to France, Coleman needed to earn more money. She left her job as a manicurist and started managing a chili parlor at Thirty-fifth Street and Indiana Avenue. Abbott gave her some money, and Jessie Binga, the rich banker and real estate broker, may also have helped her out.[8] There was also an unidentified Spaniard mentioned in a news article who may have come to her aid.[9]

Coleman started taking French language lessons at a school in the business district of Chicago. Three months later, she applied for a U.S. passport. She falsified her birth date on the application, saying she was born in 1896. That made her age twenty-four instead of twenty-eight. She also swore she had never been married. On the application, the government official described her appearance as "five feet, three and a half inches in height; a high forehead; brown skin; brown eyes; a sharp nose and medium mouth; a round chin and brown hair."[10]

John Coleman, Bessie's brother, served as a character witness for her passport, verifying that the information on the application was correct. The passport was issued on November 9, 1920. A week later, Bessie went to downtown Chicago to the British consulate's office and then the French consulate's office for tourist visas. Next, she stopped at Binga's bank on State Street near Thirty-fifth with her sister Elois to withdraw her savings for the venture. One of the officials tried to talk her out of taking the trip, saying she should leave her money in the bank.[11]

But Coleman would not abandon her dream. On November 20, 1920, she boarded the S.S. *Imperator*, a fifty-thousand-ton ocean liner. Crowds jammed onto the New York dock to throw paper streamers and shout farewells. When the ship's funnels started spewing black smoke, the stewards called for all visitors to leave the ship. Passengers waved from the promenade deck as the ship pulled away from the dock for the five-day, three-thousand-mile voyage. Steamship companies typically planned deck sports and masquerade parties to keep passengers busy on board.[12]

On November 25, 1920, the ship docked in France, and Coleman set off to learn to fly. The first school she approached was now refusing to take women because

In 1920, Coleman sailed from New York to France on the S.S. *Imperator*. In France, where flight schools accepted women and blacks, she would learn how to fly.

two had recently died in an airplane crash. She then applied to another school—École d'Aviation des Frères Caudron—and was accepted. It was located at Le Crotoy in Somme, in northern France.

This world-famous flight school was near Rouen, renowned in French history as the city where the teenage Joan of Arc gave her life rather than change her beliefs. In the fifteenth century, young Joan believed she was directed by God to lead the French army against the English invaders. She was captured and then sold to the English. They imprisoned her in an old stone tower in Rouen until she was brought to trial as a witch and a heretic. Found guilty, she was burned at the stake.

In the United States, World War I recruitment posters had used a picture of Joan of Arc to depict patriotism. Colorful posters showed her dressed in male battle gear, fighting to free her people from the invading armies. While Coleman was staying in Crotoy, the Catholic Church canonized Joan of Arc as a saint after a century-long process.

In France, Coleman walked nine miles to and from school every day for ten months. Her first flying lessons were on the ground in a French Nieuport Type 82 plane. This twenty-seven-foot biplane with a forty-foot wingspan was made of wood, lacquered cloth, pressed cardboard, wire, steel, and aluminum. It was rather flimsy, and pilots had to conduct careful inspections for any flaws that could cause parts to break off in the air.

As the trainee, Coleman sat in the rear cockpit. She was not always able to see her instructor, and she could not hear over the roar of the engine. Instead she learned by watching. This early aircraft did not have brakes or a steering wheel. A vertical stick, attached to the floor by a hinge, controlled the plane's up and down movements. Two rudder pedals caused the plane to go left or right. The instructor in the front cockpit had the same steering system. When the pilot moved his stick, Coleman would observe how her stick moved. When the pilot used one of his rudder pedals, Coleman could see one of her pedals move. She learned that a metal tailskid would drag along the ground upon touching down. The friction between the ground and the skid slowed the plane.

After some on-the-ground training, Coleman flew solo. The airplane's eighty-horsepower engine had to be primed with castor oil before it would start. When it did heat up, the strong odor of oil filled the cockpit and a yellow mist covered the pilot. The chocks that kept the plane from rolling would then be pulled away from the front wheels. The speed of ascent was controlled by the vertical stick.

Bessie Coleman had no accidents during her training period, but not all pilots were as skillful as she was. During her training, Coleman witnessed an accident in which a student pilot was killed. As a result of this accident, school officials had all the students sign a contract saying the school would not be responsible for injury or death. Coleman signed the contract, and after that she made it a practice to fly high. That way, she would have more time to correct a mechanical problem before the plane crashed to the ground.[13]

The day of the final test for her license, Coleman was shown where she must land the plane. To pass the test, she had to land within fifty meters (164 feet) of

Coleman's first flying lessons were in a flimsy Nieuport biplane. This was a popular plane used to teach pilots in France.

the spot. First, Coleman flew a five-kilometer (three-mile) closed-circuit course twice at an altitude of fifty meters. She flew a figure eight, then turned off the engine, glided into a landing, and rolled to a stop at the exact location.[14] She successfully completed the requirements to earn her pilot's license.

On June 15, 1921, eighteen years after Orville and Wilbur Wright's pioneering flight, Bessie Coleman became the first black woman in the world to earn the prestigious Fédération Aéronautique Internationale (FAI) pilot's license. Because she had been refused flying lessons in the United States, Coleman now had an international license. This document proved, without a doubt, that she was a skilled, well-trained pilot. If she had been allowed to take flying lessons in the United States, she probably would not have a license at all, because they were not required until 1926. But Coleman had followed Robert Abbott's advice and turned her disadvantages into advantages. Even Amelia Earhart, who began flying in 1921, did not have this prestigious license until two years later.

Coleman remained in France for a while, she said, because flying was so popular there. She exaggerated that "flying is as popular in Europe as automobiling is in America."[15] In Paris, she visited aircraft manufacturers and factories. She later claimed to have ordered a 130-horsepower Nieuport de Chasse to be manufactured and sent to her in the United States.

During her time in Paris, Coleman did not focus only on planes. She attended the Second Pan African Congress held in Paris at the end of the summer.[16] It was a huge gathering of leaders of African descent from all over the world and of whites who wanted to help blacks gain civil rights. Organized by William Edward Burghardt (W. E. B.) Du Bois, the Pan African Congress promoted social equality among races through education, opportunity, and conferences. The leaders of the congress believed that everything people of African heritage did—positive and negative—reflected upon the entire race. Its members maintained that all the countries with citizens of African descent were connected.

Bessie Coleman left Cherbourg, France, on September 16, 1921, on the S.S. *Manchuria*. As she disembarked in New York on September 29, reporters from both black and white newspapers rushed to her side. She dazzled and impressed them with her charm

Bessie Coleman was the first black woman in the world to earn this prestigious Fédération Aéronautique Internationale pilot's license.

and tales of adventure. Coleman knew that positive stories in the press would attract spectators to the air shows she had in mind. Perhaps also to make herself seem more interesting and glamorous, Coleman would often exaggerate. Sometimes it was difficult to tell when she was telling the truth. She often gave her age as twenty-three, even when she was much older, and she often claimed to own planes she had never purchased and embellished her experiences and accomplishments.

On this occasion, Coleman announced her plans to perform exhibition flights in the special Nieuport de Chasse plane being built for her in France. Flying in air shows with this plane, she said, she would inspire African Americans to take up aviation.[17] "We must have aviators if we are to keep up with the times," she said. "It will take courage, nerve and ambition. We have men who are physically fit; now what is needed is men who are not afraid to dare death."[18]

When a reporter asked her why she had started flying, Coleman replied that to keep pace with the times, there must be African-American aviators. She felt it was her duty to risk her life to learn aviation. Then she could encourage other African-American men and women, who were so far behind white airmen. "I made up my mind to try; I tried and was successful."[19]

While in New York, Coleman was honored at a performance of the musical hit *Shuffle Along*. After the show, the cast presented her with a silver cup engraved with their names.[20] They understood and appreciated Coleman's accomplishment. They, too, had broken through racial barriers. *Shuffle Along* was one of the first all-black musicals in New York City. It was written, produced, and directed by African Americans and starred an all-black cast.

There were no jobs for African-American pilots in the field of aviation. Barnstorming, though, had no racial restrictions. This aeronautic entertainment was

Even though Bessie Coleman had proved herself an accomplished pilot, there were no jobs available for African Americans in aviation.

also open to women. During Coleman's stay in France, Laura Brownell set a loop-the-loop record for women pilots—she flew 199 loops. Ten days after Coleman's return to Chicago, Lillian Boyer, a Chicago resident, made her first plane-to-plane transfer. Within the next year Boyer developed a stunt in which she stood in a speeding automobile and grabbed a rope ladder attached to the bottom of a plane passing overhead.

Coleman tried to buy a surplus World War I plane to participate in these exhibitions, but no one would sell her one. If she wanted to buy a plane and take lessons in stunt flying, she would have to go back to France.

5

SHOWING OFF

Bessie Coleman's dreams went far beyond just becoming a barnstormer. Five months after returning to the United States, she told a *Chicago Defender* reporter that she planned to start an aviation school. First, she would visit France to purchase planes. Upon her return, she would perform exhibitions from New York City to the aviation fields at Mineola, Long Island. Then, anyone interested in learning how to fly could attend the New York branch of her aviation school.

Coleman, who was being interviewed at her aunt's home in Harlem, New York, invited the reporter to come listen to her speak at the Metropolitan Baptist Church. Alderman George W. Harris introduced her. He told of her European achievements, then announced that she had been admitted to membership into the famous Aero Club of France in Paris.

Coleman advanced to the podium and explained her plans to open an aviation school after she picked up her plane in France. The African-American congregation honored her with a standing ovation.[1]

This time Bessie Coleman sailed on the S.S. *Paris* to France. The ship docked in Le Havre on February 28, 1922. Coleman used Europe as a stage to flaunt her piloting skills. In Amsterdam, she called on Anthony H. G. Fokker, a world-famous airplane manufacturer and stunt pilot. He invited her to visit his factory. After this visit, Coleman told reporters that Fokker had promised to build planes in the United States. She said he also agreed to set up an aviation school that would be open to all races.[2]

In an area outside Berlin, Coleman flew over the palace of the defeated kaiser in Potsdam. America's Pathé News photographers filmed the flight. Later, back in the United States, she showed this newsreel when she lectured about aviation. Coleman told reporters that she had flown a 220-horsepower Benz-motored LFG-Roland plane, the largest plane ever piloted by a woman.[3] She said that newspapers in Friedrichshafen, Germany, praised her exceptional skill in maneuvering a Dornier flying boat. She told a reporter for *The New York Times* that she test piloted this large plane.[4] The flying boat was one of the earliest types of aircraft designed to carry large numbers of passengers. It was big, heavy, and powerful.

The only negative comments published about Coleman while she was in Europe expressed disapproval of her unladylike behavior. Reporters said she should not be at the controls of such large aircraft.[5] Still, the praise outweighed the criticism. Coleman's grace and charm, and her ease with these cumbersome planes, amazed everyone.

Like the unlicensed World War I pilots back in the United States, Coleman learned to transform basic flying techniques into a magician's showmanship. She became skilled at producing illusions of danger. For example, turning off the engine before landing made it look as though the plane would crash. Audiences perceived this as a difficult trick, but really it was the first safety maneuver a pilot learned in basic training. It was used for emergency landings in the event of engine failure, an empty fuel tank, wing damage, or other unexpected hazards. The figure eights, loop-the-loops, and trick climbs performed by barnstormers were maneuvers that World War I pilots used to escape enemy fire.

During her three months in Europe, Coleman established her credibility, connections, and fame. She was fully prepared to raise the money for her aviation school by becoming a barnstormer.

When Coleman arrived in New York on August 13, 1922, she used her good looks, sense of theater, and eloquence to charm the waiting reporters. Once again Coleman showed documentation of her exploits but exaggerated details of her stories. She casually added a fictitious event that may have linked her in people's minds with Amelia Earhart, though the two pilots had never met. Reports of Earhart's setting a new women's altitude record of fourteen thousand feet had made headlines in the newspapers. The public knew that Earhart had spent World War I as a nursing aide in a military hospital. Coleman now claimed to have learned her piloting skills after going to France with a Red Cross unit during the war.[6]

Coleman showed the newsmen a letter from German ace Captain Keller, who praised her for unusual skill in piloting the LFG-Roland.[7] Coleman said she had taken lessons from Robert Thelen, the ninth pilot in Germany to receive a pilot's license. She once again brought up the subject of her aviation school, saying that Thelen had promised to deliver thirteen LFG-Rolands with 160-horsepower engines.[8] (There is no evidence that any planes were ever ordered or delivered.)

The day after Coleman returned, *The New York Times* printed an article about her. It called her the best flyer that leading French and Dutch aviators had ever seen.[9]

Robert Abbott immediately began to promote Coleman's flying exhibitions. He used the New York office of the *Chicago Defender* as headquarters for booking her barnstorming performances. Coleman and Abbott's staff designed her premier performance. She combined patriotism, African-American nationalism, and aviation. Her first show would honor the men of the segregated 15th Black Infantry Regiment, the first African-American regiment sent to France during World War I. Before joining the army, many of these men were musicians and theater performers. The regiment's brass jazz band, famous throughout Europe, would play for the audiences while Coleman flew. Coleman, the star, was billed as "The World's Greatest Woman Flyer," and the *Chicago Defender* said she was being sponsored by the "world's greatest weekly."[10]

A *Chicago Defender* article subtitled "Chicago Aviatrix to Show New Yorkers How She Does Her Stuff" gave the location and time of the event. It would be held at Glenn Curtiss Field in Garden City, Long Island, on August 27, 1922. Glenn Curtiss, who owned the field, had won the first aviators' competition against France and had been a prominent figure in aviation experimentation for many years. Now he manufactured planes and ran a school. The article

"We must have aviators if we are to keep up with the times," said Coleman. She planned to start a flying school for African Americans.

implied that Coleman would fly her own plane. It reported that she had brought a Fokker C-2 from Holland. Coleman told the reporter that several other machines had been ordered for instruction purposes and that European pilots would be brought in to teach.[11] The planes and instructors never materialized.

Because of rain, Coleman's first show in New York was rescheduled for Labor Day, when, the *Chicago Defender* reported, "the wonderful little woman" would do "heart-thrilling stunts."[12]

Bessie Coleman performed the first public flight by an African-American woman in the United States on September 3, 1922. The show began with a man from the Curtiss company, Captain Edward C. McVey, escorting Coleman to her plane and then climbing into the passenger seat. Glenn Curtiss required an employee to fly with Coleman to make sure she knew how to handle the borrowed Curtiss plane. Coleman was fashionably dressed in a tailored officer's uniform made especially for her shows. Her goggles were pushed up over her leather pilot's helmet, allowing the crowd to see her face. First she knelt in the grass beside the plane to pray. Then three thousand spectators stood, hats in hand, as the band played "The Star-Spangled Banner." The last notes of the anthem died away, and the crowd remained standing as the biplane took off. It spiraled upward into the sky. Then it traced the path of a rising half loop while banking—tilting as

Before takeoff, Coleman always inspected her plane carefully for flaws that could cause problems in the air.

it turned. Several minutes later, Coleman landed and Captain McVey climbed out.

The spectators thought the show was over, but Coleman surprised them by picking up African-American stuntman Hubert Fauntleroy Julian. He flew with her to fifteen hundred feet, then flamboyantly parachuted from the wing of the airplane. The onlookers went wild. They had just witnessed the first solo flight of an African-American woman pilot. After a smooth landing, Captain McVey presented Coleman with a flower bouquet. She concluded the show by taking individual passengers up in the plane for a $5 fee.[13]

The New York entertainment newspaper *Billboard* reported that as a pilot, Coleman was conservative but skilled. Officials at the field praised her ability to pilot a plane she had no prior experience with. *Billboard* also reported that more African Americans probably flew that day than had flown since planes were invented.[14]

Coleman performed no stunts at this performance because Glenn Curtiss did not allow stunts. Even so, young African Americans phoned Coleman's office after the show, seeking information on how to become pilots. She told them that there would not be a training school unless people helped by donating money for it. Or interested students could wait until she had raised enough money by barnstorming.[15]

6

CRASHING IN
CALIFORNIA

wo thousand spectators attended Bessie
Coleman's Chicago debut on October 15,
1922. Adults paid $1, and children paid
twenty-five cents to see what the *Chicago Defender* billed
as a "Daredevil Aviatrix" in "Hair-Raising Stunts."
Susan Coleman sat in this audience. She came to see
her daughter fly an airplane, to witness the
performance by the daughter she had raised on
African-American pride, book learning, and faith in
God. Beside Susan Coleman sat Bessie's sisters, nieces,
and nephew.

Once again, Coleman draped her performance in

patriotism. This time she was honoring the regiment her brothers had joined, the 8th Infantry Regiment of the Illinois National Guard. This segregated regiment had been the second National Guard unit to be shipped to France and was the only one that commissioned African-American officers.

Coleman wove the patriotic theme into her flying. The program included maneuvers named after World War I fighter pilots. The advertisement in the *Chicago Defender* stated she would start with a maneuver called the French Nungesser takeoff. It was named for pilot Charles Eugene J. M. Nungesser, who had shot down forty-five planes during World War I by flying close to the ground. Next she would demonstrate a strategy used by Eddie Rickenbacker, a famous American World War I ace who had twenty-six victories in plane fights against the Germans. These stunts and others had been used by war pilots to dodge bullets fired from stationary guns on enemy planes.

Again, the show began with Coleman kneeling in prayer beside a borrowed plane. The owner of the Checkerboard Airdrome, David L. Behncke, had provided the plane. After the playing of "The Star-Spangled Banner," Coleman's plane eased into the air but stayed near the ground. There, Coleman gracefully performed low-level aerobatics. Next she dipped the plane dangerously close to the audience. Jazzy patriotic music played by the 8th Infantry Band

BESSIE COLEMAN

THE RACE'S ONLY

AVIATRIX

WILL MAKE HER INITIAL
LOCAL FLIGHT AT

CHECKERBOARD AIRDROME

SUNDAY, OCT. 15

3 P. M. SHARP

DIRECTIONS
METROPOLITAN "L"—Garfield Park
to Forest Park station; motor bus
to field.
AUTO ROUTE—West on Jackson Blvd.
to Desplaines Ave., south to Roose-
velt Road, west three blocks to
Checkerboard Airdrome.

SEE THIS DAREDEVIL AVIATRIX

IN HER

HAIR-RAISING STUNTS

Including French Nungesser Take-off, Spanish Berta Costa Climb,
American Curtis-McMullen Turn, Eddie Rickenbacker Straighten-up,
Richtofen German Glide, Ralph C. Diggins Landing. Presentation of
Honor Flag to 8th Ill. Infantry. Wing Walking and Parachute Jumps

FOUR SEPARATE FLIGHTS

AND SPECIAL PASSENGER CARRYING

Admission: Children, 25 Cents. Adults, $1.00

For her first airshow in Chicago, Coleman promised wing walking, parachute jumps, and other amazing stunts. "At first I was a curiosity," said Coleman, "but soon the public discovered I could really fly."

enhanced the drama. Then came the Spanish Bertha Coast climb. Immediately, she veered off into an American Curtis McMullen turn. The audience sighed with relief as she straightened into the Eddie Rickenbacker move. She ended with the Baron Manfred von Richthofen (the Red Baron) glide and the Ralph C. Diggins landing, which was a level glide.

After intermission, Colonel Otis B. Duncan, commander of the 8th Illinois infantry, walked Coleman to her plane. The crowd burst into applause as he joined her in the cockpit and they took off. Coleman climbed, then flew in a figure eight in honor of Duncan and his regiment. The plane seemed to be out of control as it turned and twisted back toward earth. When Coleman righted the plane, the crowd sighed with relief. She continued the show by banking, making several low dips, then gliding into a smooth landing.

The third part of show was supposed to involve Bessie's sister Georgia, adorned in red, white, and blue. Bessie had advertised one detail that she had forgotten to tell her sister. She expected Georgia to parachute to the ground from two thousand feet in the air. But Georgia had no intention of jumping. When Georgia heard Bessie's plan, the sisters argued. Then in unison they laughed and repeated a line of poetry they used to recite together as children, "Uh, uh, not me."[1]

Georgia did not jump from the plane, but Coleman flew several figure eights in the air, then landed. She ended the exhibition by presenting the regiment with a white satin honor flag with the number 8 appliquéd to it. After the show, Coleman, Behncke, and other pilots gave rides until dark.[2]

A *Chicago Defender* reporter wrote that the audience was not disappointed: "They witnessed the most marvelous flying feats ever performed by the most daring aviators. . . . Bessie Coleman performed beyond the ability of the average aviator. She was successful in every way."[3] Still, he said, even with all her fame, Coleman was the same unassuming, friendly woman she had always been.

Coleman may have seemed unassuming to the reporter, but the Seminole Film Producing Company did not find her to be so pleasant. This African-American company wanted to make a feature-length movie about her. The film was to star Coleman, and the cast would include twelve other actors and one hundred extras. Bessie Coleman signed a contract.

On the first day of shooting, the producer told Coleman to dress like a poor ignorant girl arriving in New York. She refused. As a child, she had vowed to herself and family that she would never be like the helpless characters in the 1852 novel *Uncle Tom's Cabin* by Harriet Beecher Stowe. She intended to keep that promise. She told the producer, "No Uncle Tom stuff for me!"[4] Then she walked out. Six automobiles packed with people associated with the movie were waiting at the airport to film a scene. Coleman never showed up. Instead she left for Baltimore without informing anyone on the movie set.

In Baltimore, Coleman announced to reporters that she had opened a school for aviators at 628 Indiana Avenue in Chicago.[5] But an office alone was not a complete flying school. She could teach *about* flying, but she still needed a plane and a hangar to fulfill her dream. This would require much more money. She asked one of her African-American students, Robert Paul Sachs, if his company would hire her to drop advertisements from a plane. Sachs, a midwestern advertising manager for the Coast Tire and Rubber Company, suggested she go to the company's headquarters in Oakland, California, to see if this would be possible.

Arriving by train in California, Coleman went directly to the Coast Tire and Rubber Company. She described the factory to reporters as the best-equipped, most modern plant she had ever seen. She also told them that her school would be in Oakland.[6]

Next, Coleman went to the coastal area of southern California, which had been a favorite place for aviators for many years. It had a steady sea breeze and mild weather. Glenn Curtiss had a school on North Island near San Diego that he had started in 1911. North Island also had many army surplus planes.

Rockwell Army Intermediate Depot on North Island at Coronado stored several of these planes because the United States had overproduced them during World War I. After the war, France and England had returned their surplus planes to the United States. Then the two European countries set up embargoes. This meant that only a limited number of the planes could be imported into their countries. Consequently, the United States had an abundance of planes to sell.

Fifty planes, disassembled and packed in their original crates, were for sale at the Rockwell depot. Coleman bought a surplus biplane for $400. Made by the Curtiss company, the plane was the fourth design of the JN model, nicknamed the "Jenny." There was nothing fancy about this type of plane. It did not have the power and prestige of the planes she had flown in Europe.

The first Jennies were built in 1914, but they lacked speed and were difficult to maneuver. Curtiss made different models, the Model J and the Model N. Then he blended the best features of both into the JN. He kept improving the design until he was happy with it. Like Henry Ford's Model T, which allowed people without a lot of money to enjoy the thrill of driving, the JN-4 made it possible for everyday people to fly.

After the war, 95 percent of the pilots in the United States took their flying lessons in this plane. It weighed 1,430 pounds. Its one engine, called an OX-5, was water-cooled and had ninety horsepower.

The Jenny was not a safe vehicle. It was not uncommon for the engine's camshaft to shatter in flight. The outside hoses would leak and come loose, spewing hot water. The OX-5 was so undependable that one pilot joked, "Some of the horses were usually limping."[7] Other pilots said the Jenny was just a bunch of parts flying in formation.

Knowing its unpredictable nature, pilots devised a safe way to crash-land it. They would aim the Jenny between two trees. When the plane hit the trees, its wooden wings would splinter and fold back. The fuselage would not be damaged, and the pilot could walk away with only a few bruises.

Coleman told reporters that she had ordered two more planes besides her Jenny. One was for the president of the Coast Tire and Rubber Company; the other was for the company's advertising director.[8] Coleman explained that these men were purchasing the planes so that they could take lessons from her.

After Coleman's plane had been assembled, she wanted her first West Coast exhibition to be at Rogers Field in Los Angeles. That was where Amelia Earhart had flown. Finding out it was not available, Coleman agreed to participate in a fairground's opening celebration at Palomar Park near Slauson Avenue in Santa Monica, California.

On February 4, 1923, Bessie Coleman climbed into her very own plane to fly to Santa Monica, twenty miles away. Once the propeller started turning and the chocks next to the front wheels were removed, Coleman gave a thumbs-up. She started off directly into the wind, staying on the ground until maximum speed was reached. Finally she easily and smoothly took off. She made a steady climb at forty miles an hour. At three hundred feet, the engine stalled. According to witnesses, "the motor of her plane lost its rhythmic drone, sputtered, and two cylinders went dead."[9]

Coleman tried to bring the plane level so it could glide down, but she dropped too fast. The plane dived, and the nose hit the ground full force, shattering the propeller into splinters and burying the engine nearly three feet into the soft soil. Coleman, unconscious, had to be cut out of the tangled wreckage.

Coleman was rushed to St. Catherine's Hospital in Santa Monica. She told the field manager that she would be back later, but as it turned out, her injuries were too extensive for her to return to the show that day. The doctor set a double fracture in her left leg and then fitted her with a full cast, from ankle to hip. Coleman also had three broken ribs and multiple cuts.[10]

As Coleman was being settled into the hospital bed, ten thousand people at Palamor Park were wondering when she would gallantly fly onto the fairgrounds. As they waited, unaware of the crash, anger spread through the crowd. Some demanded refunds. A few

The early biplanes had no brakes or steering wheels, and accidents were all too common.

called the exhibition a fraud. After they learned of the accident, some said she deserved it because she had flown on a Sunday.[11] Others considered the accident to be part of a conspiracy. The *Chicago Defender* suggested that it could have been caused by some white mechanics who may have tampered with the steering apparatus in an effort to keep her from gaining the recognition due her.[12]

Whatever the cause, the crash did not stop Bessie Coleman. Instead, she saw it as a victory for flying. Her being alive proved that flying was no more dangerous than riding in an automobile. She sent the following telegram to friends and well-wishers: "Tell them all that as soon as I can walk I'm going to fly!" She also wrote that she had not lost her faith in aviation as a way to help African Americans fulfill their destiny.[13]

Coleman stayed in the hospital for three months. During this time, the *California Eagle* newspaper printed a letter from Robert Sachs. He requested that people send money to help in her worthy effort of trying to open an aviation school. Employees at his company had sent donations to the school because they felt a personal interest in Coleman. She had volunteered to distribute Coast Tire and Rubber advertisements from the air.[14]

Bessie Coleman did not wait for donations. She placed a detailed ad in the *California Eagle* promoting the Coleman School of Aeronautics. Tuition would be

$400, with $25 paid at contract signing, the rest to be paid in installments. In return, she promised quality instructors and equipment. At the time, though, she had neither.[15]

A month after the accident, Coleman gave an interview to a *Chicago Defender* reporter. It was the first time she voiced her annoyance with African Americans for not contributing to the proposed school. She dramatically asked the newspaper's readers, "Must I escape from death to open a school for whites only?" Then she complained that seven African-Americans had expressed an interest learning to fly, but no African Americans would provide them with the money needed to do so. The reporter tried to soften Coleman's words by telling of her frustration with those who had not given her financial support. Coleman, he explained, felt alone in the project and fearful that her people would not grasp this valuable opportunity. She ended the interview by saying there were no African Americans at Rockwell Field except a seventy-eight-year-old man—and he was there to pick up the paper wrappings torn from the new engines. "Isn't that a shame?" she asked.[16]

Bessie Coleman hobbled out of the hospital on crutches on May 10, 1923. Her lower hip was bandaged, and a cast encased her leg. Newspaper boys on street corners hawked newspapers with articles about the first nonstop transcontinental flight from

To raise money to buy herself an airplane, Coleman helped advertise tires for the Coast Tire and Rubber Company.

Hempstead, New York, to San Diego, California, by Oakley G. Kelly and John A. Macready. The trip took 26 hours, 50 minutes, and 38 seconds and covered 2,530 miles at an average speed of 99 miles an hour.

Coleman recuperated at a friend's house in Los Angeles. In the evenings, she gave lectures at the YMCA. At fifty cents for an adult and thirty-five cents for a child, the patrons got their money's worth. They watched the twenty-minute Pathé News film showing Coleman flying an LFG in Germany over the kaiser's palace, as well as her other flights in Europe.[17] Her fans also got to see her in a newspaper ad in which she posed with a huge tire as the "Business Booster" for the Coast Tire and Rubber Company.[18]

7

TAKING CHARGE

itizens of Columbus, Ohio, looked forward to a spectacular exhibition on Labor Day in 1923. The air show would feature the feats of Bessie Coleman as well as stunt performers "Daredevil Erwin" and Iona McCarthy. Coleman received a letter from the mayor of the city, who wrote, "Being familiar with your career and the skill, daring and courage you have exhibited on so many occasions and knowing how your efforts have been recognized by the heads of many European governments, I deem it an honor and a privilege to welcome you to the city of Columbus."[1]

The show was delayed because of rain. Coleman

waited at Driving Park, hoping for clear skies. On the other side of the park, two thousand members of the Ku Klux Klan—in white robes and hoods—gathered for a picnic to welcome new members.[2] The hate group targeted blacks, Catholics, and Jews, and its membership was growing.

The rain continued and the show had to be postponed. Coleman went back to Chicago. There, according to the *Chicago Defender*, she promised to perform, saying that she was expecting a plane to be delivered. She even announced that it would be exhibited at the 8th Regiment Armory.[3] A plane never arrived, but she did return to Columbus to perform.

On September 9, 1923, ten thousand spectators cheered as Coleman circled, rolled, and dived in a borrowed plane. The crowd stomped and whistled as Daredevil Erwin hung from a plane by a leather strap clenched in his teeth. Next, Iona McCarthy performed an amazing stunt using three parachutes.[4]

Coleman's exhibition was a success, but she still had no plane of her own, and no manager—and no more bookings. Because of her strong-willed, independent personality, she had fired or lost five managers.[5]

Coleman decided it was time to take a good long rest.[6] She took her furniture out of storage and settled in an apartment at Forty-second and South Parkway in Chicago. There she visited with friends. She also cooked large meals for her nieces and nephew and let them play music on her windup Victrola record player. Sunday matinees at the Peerless Theater replaced her flying at the Airdrome.[7]

In the evenings Coleman attended jazz clubs such as the Dreamland. She wore elegant beaded gowns that she had bought in Paris and wigs curled in fashionable styles. On the arm of rich, influential escorts, she gracefully walked down the Stroll. Men of all nationalities came to the apartment to court her. "She was a pretty woman and she took advantage of it," said her niece Marion.[8]

Prince Kojo Tovalou-Houénou became one of her companions.[9] His father, the king of Dahomey (now Benin), Africa, had been forced out of his country by the French. Prince Kojo served as the head of Marcus Garvey's Universal Negro Improvement Association (UNIA). This group believed that dark skin color was a sign of strength and beauty. The UNIA promoted racial pride and said that blacks should leave the United States because it was a white man's country where a black person could not be successful.

Prince Kojo was a showman just like Bessie Coleman. At formal gatherings he would wear elaborate costumes. He spread Garvey's belief that African Americans should return to Africa and set up their own independent nation. Copper-skinned Coleman also promoted racial pride, but she believed that African Americans should fight for equal rights while living and working beside whites. Coleman's relationship with Prince Kojo did not last long.

Bessie Coleman could not stay on the ground for too long. In May 1925, she left Chicago and returned to her home state of Texas. In Houston, she established an exhibition headquarters. Then she joined the Theater Owners Booking Association, known as TOBA. This group, which provided entertainment bookings, arranged for Coleman to lecture at African-American theaters, schools, and churches. Coleman talked about the value of aviation.

Informally, performers said the letters TOBA stood for "Tough On Black Actors" because bookings were scheduled mainly in the segregated South. There, the Jim Crow laws defined what African Americans could or could not do. Black entertainers could not eat in whites-only restaurants, stay in whites-only hotels, or use whites-only public rest rooms. Often, after a performance, they had to drive through the night to get to the next town in time for their booking.[10]

Coleman used her lectures to promote her school for African-American pilots, but she also had another motivation. She wanted to change the way southerners treated African Americans. She wanted her people to stand up to the Jim Crow laws. She had told a reporter for the *California Eagle* that her "great ambition" was "to make Uncle Tom's cabin into a hangar by establishing a flying school."[11] In the book she had read as a child, the cabin where Uncle Tom lived was a place where other slaves gathered. Coleman wanted her flying school to be a gathering place for African Americans.

On June 19, 1925, Coleman demonstrated the freedom of flying by performing on Juneteenth, the day commemorating the end of slavery in Texas. Newspaper reports called this event "Bessie Coleman's Flying Circus." She made her show as exciting as the Ringling Brothers Circus she had attended as a child in Waxahachie. She filled the exhibition with music, suspense, and illusions. Only, unlike the magicians in the circus, Coleman had no trapdoor to escape through. Her tricks were more dangerous. In her patriotic uniform, Coleman appeared to have been transformed into a confident military pilot. The jazz group's music introduced her with a fanfare and added a sense of importance to the occasion. This show was so successful that Coleman scheduled more shows throughout Texas.

Coleman performed in Austin, where she also met Miriam A. Ferguson, one of the first women governors in the United States.[12] "Ma" Ferguson had a reputation for being tough on the Ku Klux Klan. She was also known for granting a high number of pardons and paroles to convicts, many of whom were black.

In Wharton, Texas, Coleman hired Elizia Delworth to parachute from the wing of her plane. During

Coleman's exhibition on August 9, 1925, Delworth backed out of the stunt. Local newspapers later complained that Coleman had not delivered what she promised. On Sunday, Coleman performed in Wharton again. This time she did the jump herself. After the stunt-flying portion of the show, another pilot took the controls of the plane. At two thousand feet, Coleman crawled out of the cockpit and moved toward the back edge of the wing. She fastened the jumper-harness straps of her parachute, then plummeted off. Always the exhibitionist, Coleman landed right in the middle of the audience.[13]

The Memphis, Tennessee, exhibition at the annual state fair was almost Coleman's last. Her plane slowly climbed into the air, and just as Coleman began a loop, the engine faltered. She circled back toward the field and landed without difficulty. Most of the spectators had no idea how close they had come to seeing a disaster. But a young boy approached Coleman to ask if her engine had failed. Coleman was surprised that he had noticed. She told the boy that he was right. Proud of his observation, the boy smiled smugly.[14]

Coleman scheduled lectures at schools, churches, and movie theaters because it was less expensive than doing air shows. Donations for her school were collected at these events.

The day after a lecture in Dallas, Texas, Coleman paid the twenty-five-cent fare for a bus ride past cotton fields and ranches to Love Airfield outside Dallas. Love Field, like Rockwell Field in Coronado, sold biplanes. Coleman's attention was drawn to a Curtiss JN—a Jenny like the one she had purchased in California. Unfortunately, she could not afford the servicing it needed.[15]

Coleman's next exhibition was in Waxahachie, where she had grown up. Citizens on the east side of the train tracks knew her as the top seller of tickets for a church bazaar, as the girl who brought home a band. West side residents may have recognized her as the back-door laundress. Now she was returning to her hometown world-renowned as the first African-American woman pilot.

Bessie Coleman promised Waxahachie that she would present the greatest show on earth. It would be held on the grounds of Trinity, the white college. Advertisements were printed and posted. Tickets were sold. It was decided that African Americans could attend, and arrangements were made so they would have their own entrance. But when Coleman heard this, she refused to perform. She demanded that blacks and whites of Waxahachie be permitted to use the same door. If not, she would pack up and leave. The authorities gave in. There would be just one entrance, but seating would be segregated.[16]

Coleman traveled widely to spread the word about her aeronautical adventures. She showed her film,

COMING SOON!

D. IRELAND THOMAS
PRESENTS

MISS BESSIE COLEMAN

The Only Colored Girl Aviatrix In The World.

In Person and on the Screen, showing her flights in Europe and America and her accident while flying in California.

Being impossible to fly in every City or Town, Miss Coleman is bringing her flights to you in Motion Pictures and appearing in person at every showing. Join the mighty throng and see the idol of the race; greet her. Shake her hand as she has blazed a new trail for the race. Come early as every one will be there to see the little girl who has the nerve to fly.

After flying in Europe. Miss Coleman has made successful flights in New York, Columbus, Ohio, Los Angeles, Cal., Memphis, Tenn., Etc.

Coleman traveled throughout the South, giving lectures and showing her film at African-American theaters, schools, and churches.

asked for donations, and recruited students for her aviation school. Back in Chicago, her agent, D. Ireland Thomas, set up a series of lectures for her at black theaters in Georgia and Florida.

On Christmas Eve, Coleman unexpectedly arrived at Elois's house with bags packed for Savannah, Georgia. The sisters made presents and wrapped them. Elois hemmed a black taffeta dress for Bessie. They sipped coffee and talked till morning. On Christmas Day at dawn, Bessie left. This would be the last time Elois would see her.[17]

Coleman lectured in Savannah, Augusta, and Atlanta, Georgia. In Florida she spoke at the Liberty Theater in St. Petersburg and in theaters in Tampa and West Palm Beach.

It seemed as if 1926 would be the year the Coleman Aeronautical School would finally be established. Coleman wrote optimistic letters to Elois, detailing her progress. She reported that once she even took an escort and went into a poolroom to talk to African-American men about aviation.[18]

Coleman stayed in Orlando with the Reverend Hezakiah Keith Hill, of the Mount Zion Missionary Baptist Institutional Church, and his wife, Viola, They treated her like family. During this time, she became a born-again Christian.[19]

Everywhere Coleman went, she used her influence to try to correct injustices. After the all-white Orlando

Chamber of Commerce had booked Coleman for a parachute jump, she discovered that African Americans would not be allowed to attend. She threatened to send her plane back to Texas in protest. The chamber of commerce, unaware that she did not own a plane, took her threat seriously and agreed to let African Americans attend. Then Coleman pushed

"The sky is the only place where there is no prejudice. Up there, everyone is equal. Everyone is free," said Bessie Coleman.

even further. She insisted that pamphlets be dropped by plane to inform the African-American community that segregation laws were being lifted for this event.[20] It was a brave stand for Coleman to take. Segregation practices were very strict in some Florida towns, where African Americans had to carry a special pass even to be out after dark.[21]

Feeling confident, Bessie Coleman once again attempted to have a movie made about her life. At the suggestion, she said, of Mr. Trumbull, the owner of the Liberty Theater in St. Petersburg, she wrote to Norman Studios in Arlington, Florida, on February 3, 1926. R. E. Norman, a white man, was an independent director. He made films that featured positive images of African Americans on screen. Coleman explained what she had in mind. "I have titled my play 'Yesterday—Today & Tomorrow.'"[22]

Norman replied that he was very interested in such a film. He believed that it would attract African-American audiences. He said it would be five or six reels long, and Coleman would play the lead. Then he asked about her plans for the project.

Having no money to produce the film, Coleman responded by assuring Norman that it would draw African Americans to the theater and make money. She told him that the showing of her newsreels drew more audiences than some of the dramas featured at the theaters. She asked him to help finance the movie. In response, he told her agent that to make a good film would cost $4,000 to $5,000 but that he did not want to put up the money. The film was never made.

After this disappointment, Viola Hill offered to help Coleman open a beauty shop in Orlando. Air shows and lectures would not bring in enough money to open an aviation school. By styling hair and manicuring nails, said Hill, Coleman could make a steady income to finance a school.[23] Coleman wrote to Elois, "I am on the threshold of opening a school."[24]

Coleman was asked by the Negro Welfare League in Jacksonville, Florida, to perform at its 1926 First of May Field Day. Coleman was delighted to be invited by an African-American group, but she could not locate a plane that she could use in Florida. No one in the area would sell, rent, or lend a plane to an African American.[25]

Coleman did not give up. She knew that Edwin M. Beeman, one of Florida's most prominent men, admired her bravery. He agreed to pay $500 for Coleman to have a plane transported from Dallas to Jacksonville.[26] This white benefactor was the son of Harry L. Beeman, millionaire manufacturer of Beeman Chewing Gum. Coleman ordered a plane from the Curtiss Southwestern Airplane and Motor Company in Dallas. For the first time since her California accident, Coleman would be performing in her own plane.

Coleman promised the Hills, who had grown to think of her as a daughter, that this would be her last dangerous performance. After this, she assured them, she would stick to giving lectures. On April 27, 1926, Coleman boarded a train for Jacksonville, Florida.

8

GAMBLING WITH DEATH

essie Coleman's plane was delivered on Wednesday, April 28, 1926, in Jacksonville. The only plane Coleman could afford was another Jenny biplane. Because it was so old, its engine had not been maintained. The plane could develop only sixty horsepower instead of its ninety-horsepower potential.[1]

Twenty-four-year-old William Wills, a white mechanic and an employee of the Curtiss company, flew the plane to Coleman. He was supposedly a veteran of sixty-seven flights, but this had been a difficult trip. He had been forced to make two emergency stops in Mississippi on his way to Jacksonville.

Despite the poor condition of the plane, Coleman still intended to fly it for the May 1 event. She also planned to make a parachute jump. The fairgrounds were ready. The Ferris wheel had been newly painted. Tables for the pitchers of pink lemonade and hot dogs lined the sawdust area. The Elite Circle and Girls Deluxe Club had hung banners in honor of Coleman. These decorations advertised "An Aerial Frolic," a dance to be held the night of her performance.[2]

The publicity manager for the Negro Welfare League, John Betsch, scheduled Coleman to speak at a school the morning before the exhibition. Coleman, dressed in her smart flying uniform, encouraged African-American students to consider careers in aviation.

After her talk Coleman entered a restaurant, where she spied Robert Abbott. She was surprised and delighted to see the *Chicago Defender* owner. "This is the man who gave me my chance. I shall never forget him," she said.[3] Abbott, like a protective father, warned Coleman that he did not like the looks of William Wills. He warned her not to go up in a plane with the Texan.

That evening, Coleman spoke at the Strand Theater. She passionately expressed her dream to improve the lives of African-Americans by training them for the field of aviation.

The following morning, Friday, April 30, at 6:30 A.M., John Betsch and Bessie Coleman picked up

The Elite Circle and Girls DeLuxe Club
expect you and your friends to enjoy
"An Aerial Frolic"
honoring
Miss Bessie Coleman
Sat. May 1. 8:30 to 12 P. M.   Pythian Auditorium
Subscription 75c
Music by the Imperial Jazz Orchestra

"An Aerial Frolic"—a dance to honor Bessie Coleman—was planned for the evening of her air show in Jacksonville, Florida.

William Wills to go to Paxon Field for a practice flight. They arrived at the sixty-acre private field at 7:15. Beside her very own plane, Coleman knelt in prayer. As she climbed into the cockpit, she promised Betsch that she would take him up for a ride later.[4]

William Wills sat in the front cockpit at the controls; Coleman sat in the back. She did not fasten her seatbelt. This would allow her to lean over the side of the plane to find a suitable landing spot for the parachute jump.

Wills took the Jenny toward the racetrack, climbed to 3,500 feet, then circled back to Paxon Field. According to Betsch, who watched from the field below, "They'd been up twelve minutes and had reached 3,000 feet when something went wrong. They had done a nose dive, but instead of righting the plane, it plunged right on down."[5]

Bessie Coleman fell out of the plane at two thousand feet in the air. She hit the ground so hard that her leather leggings burst open. Nearly every bone in her body was crushed.

After Coleman's fall, Wills tried to straighten the plane, but it continued downward end over end. It sheared off the top of a pine tree, then crashed. The farmland where the plane fell was owned by Mrs. W. L. Meadows. Her son, Raymond, called the police. Mrs. Meadows and a friend were unable to pull Wills's body free because the plane was too heavy to lift.

John Betsch raced to the scene, arriving at the same time as the police. Nervous and upset, Betsch lit a cigarette. A spark ignited gasoline fumes from the plane, and Coleman's fragile wood-framed Jenny biplane burned like tinder. A policeman tried to rescue Wills, but the flames were too intense. The officer's trousers caught fire. Wills, trapped inside, was cremated.[6]

The police arrested Betsch and took him to jail. He was released after several hours of questioning. The police concluded that the fire had been an accident. They believed that Betsch, confused and upset because of the crash, did not think before lighting the match.

Once the wreckage had cooled, souvenir seekers tore at Coleman's plane. The *Chicago Defender* ran photographs of the smashed and charred aircraft. Clippings were posted in the windows of Chicago's South Side stores. The newspaper headline said, "Girl Flyer Is Killed in Plane Fall."[7] The day before, a caption under Coleman's picture had stressed the danger of her flights: "Gambles with Death," it read. The *Defender* called the tragedy "one of the most sensational of all the disasters to have marred the progress of flying in this country."[8]

The Jacksonville Negro Welfare League took Bessie Coleman's battered body to undertaker Lawton L. Pratt.[9] Wills's body was taken to a funeral parlor for

Coleman fell two thousand feet to her death from the rear cockpit of her plane. Pilot William Wills died as the plane crashed to the ground.

whites. The fair was canceled. Stunt flying was prohibited at Paxon Field.

Bessie Coleman's body, clothed in a dress rather than her flying uniform, lay in state at the parlor until the funeral service on May 1. People filed past it until after midnight to pay their respects. An overflow crowd of five thousand mourners attended the service at the Bethel Baptist Church. People from all walks of life came together to honor her. Many of them paused for a moment before the open casket.[10]

On Sunday, May 2, 1926, Coleman's remains were

taken by train to Orlando, Florida. Jacksonville citizens paid the $360 cost.

In Orlando, the Reverend Hezakiah Keith Hill gave a heartfelt eulogy at the Mount Zion Missionary Baptist Institutional Church on Monday morning. He told the congregation that Coleman had become more religious during her stay with his family. He spoke of her kindness to all who knew her.[11]

Years before, family members had questioned the sacrifices Bessie would have to make to reach her goal. The soloist sang a song on that day that could easily have been Coleman's answer: "I've done my work. I've sung my song. I've done some good. I've done some wrong. And I shall go where I belong. The Lord has willed it so."[12]

The pallbearers placed the casket carrying Coleman's body into a hearse waiting outside the church. At the Illinois Central Railroad Station, more than five hundred grieving African Americans gathered. As the casket was placed aboard a baggage car bound for Chicago, the crowd hummed sweetly, "My Country 'Tis of Thee." Viola Hill accompanied the body.

On Wednesday, May 5, Chicago mourned Bessie Coleman's death. Approximately ten thousand people passed by her casket at the funeral parlor. Funeral services were held on Friday morning, May 7, at the Pilgrim Baptist Church. Thirty-five hundred mourners who could not fit into the church stood respectfully outside on the sidewalk.

Susan Coleman leaned on her son John's arm as she walked down the long church aisle to the front pews.[13] Elois, Nilus, and Georgia followed their mother. Bessie's nieces and nephew, all ten years of age and younger, did not attend. Six World War I veterans of the African-American 8th Infantry Regiment of the Illinois National Guard marched solemnly down the aisle carrying Coleman's flag-draped casket. Twenty-four honorary pallbearers followed.

Ida B. Wells-Barnett, the journalist who had become an outspoken voice against the lynchings of African Americans, led the service. She recalled how Coleman had come to her home after earning her pilot's license. She had wanted to thank Wells-Barnett for her letter of congratulations. It was the only letter Coleman had received in recognition of her achievement.

Other prominent citizens praised Coleman's unselfish courage, integrity, and intelligence. Then Colonel Otis B. Duncan reminisced about how Coleman had honored his regiment at her debut performance four years earlier in Chicago.[14]

Just before the funeral, the Reverend Junius Austin, Sr., had received a message from an African-American church member who complained that Coleman had gotten too much help from white people. Austin decided to focus on Bessie Coleman's commitment to her people.[15] Austin and the Reverend C. M. Tanner spoke about the lack of African-American support for Coleman. Austin, referring to the written complaint, said that Coleman would not have gotten as far if she had not been helped by whites. He pointed out that few successful African Americans had accomplished their goals without the help of whites. He called Coleman an African-American woman ahead of her time who was not appreciated by other African Americans. Although African Americans admired "Brave Bessie" and attended her exhibitions, few had supported her financially. If they had, she would have had enough money to buy a decent plane and start her school.[16] The minister stressed Coleman's loyalty to the African-American race. He stated that although she had been offered large amounts of money to give exhibitions exclusively for the whites, she steadily refused to accept them unless fellow blacks were also allowed admission. The choir then sang "Jesus, Savior, Pilot Me," a hymn Coleman had heard in the Baptist church she attended as a little girl in Texas.

Viola Hill, her voice breaking, spoke of Bessie Coleman's courage and unselfishness. She read a note found in Coleman's pocket at the time of her death:

> *My Dear One: I am writing you to congratulate you on your brave doings. I want to be an aviatrix when I get [to be] a woman. I like to see our own race do*

brave things. I am going to be out there to see you jump from the airplane. I want an airplane of my own when I get [to be] a woman.

Many kisses.
Yours a little girl, RUBY MAE Mc DUFFIE [17]

Lincoln Cemetery at Kedzie Avenue and 123rd Street was Bessie Coleman's final destination. African Americans had founded this cemetery in 1911 because they were not permitted to be buried in whites-only cemeteries. Far from city noises, amid tall pines and maples, the casket was lowered into the earth. "Oh Bessie, you tried so hard," sobbed her sister Georgia.[18] Sorrowing family members and friends departed Lincoln Cemetery, leaving Bessie Coleman buried in an unmarked grave.

On Memorial Day in 1927, the Cooperative Businessmen's League of Cook County and Florida Friends unveiled a plaque at Coleman's grave site. The inscription read: "In memory of Bessie Coleman, one of the first American women to enter the field of Aviation. Remembered for her courage and accomplishments. She fell 5,300 feet while flying in Jacksonville, Florida, April 30, 1926."[19] (The number of feet is incorrect.)

9

SEARCHING FOR THE TRUTH

obert Abbott's comment that he did not like the look of William Wills made people begin to wonder. Perhaps Bessie Coleman's death was not an accident. Was there a conspiracy? Was a white southerner behind it? An article in the *Baltimore Afro-American* said the accident indicated foul play.[1] The reporter wrote that Wills, an experienced pilot, may have planned to tip the plane and then right it, but his plan went wrong.

Elois Patterson, Coleman's sister, rekindled the discussion forty-three years after the accident. She said that she could not understand why Bessie did not have on her parachute. Safety first had been Bessie Coleman's motto while doing chores around the house, much less flying.[2]

There is some confusion about Wills's identity. He may not have been unknown to Coleman. Elois Patterson wrote that Coleman "trusted her companion implicitly."[3] She also referred to Wills as Coleman's publicity agent. News articles stated that he had been her mechanic. Any of these relationships would explain Coleman's trust and dampen any thoughts

In 1927, a year after Coleman's tragic death, a plaque was placed to mark her grave site.

that he had been part of a conspiracy to cause Coleman's death. Marion Coleman, Bessie's niece, identified Wills as a Frenchman who had returned with Coleman from Europe. She said he accompanied Bessie everywhere she went.[4]

Conspiracy theories died down when investigators found a wrench in the wreckage of Coleman's airplane. It had jammed into the control gears. There is no way Wills could have reached back from the cockpit to place it there. Nor could he have done so before the flight—the plane would not have been able to fly.

Investigators concluded that Wills, a mechanic and also an experienced pilot, had accidentally left the wrench somewhere near the control gears. After take-off, when the plane tipped, the wrench slid into the gears.[5] There is no way to know whether he purposely tipped the plane to cause Bessie's accident or whether he had a disastrous careless moment. As Marion Coleman said, "There are always those that try to make it more than it was."[6]

10

LEADING THE WAY

essie Coleman was an African-American pioneer in the field of aviation. She blazed a trail that many have followed. Immediately after her death, her contributions to aviation were recognized. *The Norfolk Journal and Guide* praised Coleman for teaching women that they could fly.[1] A *Dallas Express* editorial discussed her major contribution to African Americans.[2]

The thousands of mourners who attended her funerals were proof that she had made an impression on the lives of many. Coleman gave African Americans strength and hope. The editor of the *Chicago Defender*,

Enoch P. Waters, said that an African-American woman flying was close to being a miracle.[3] It was an extraordinary achievement.

In 1927, amid all the publicity and excitement of Charles Lindbergh's solo flight from New York to Paris, Bessie Coleman once again made the papers. *The New York News* in Harlem, New York, sponsored a contest to name an apartment building at 140th Street in Harlem. Mrs. Nellie Harrison was the winner with her suggestion that they honor Bessie Coleman, and the apartments were given the name Coleman Manor

Harrison called Coleman the black Joan of Arc. New York City had just proclaimed Colonel Lindbergh its hero, she said, so it would be only right to name the apartment building after the African-American flier, "our deceased female eagle of the air."[4] Bessie's sister Elois agreed: Lindbergh and Coleman both completed important missions. Lindbergh's was to be the first pilot to fly to Paris nonstop from New York. Coleman's mission was to bring the art of flying to African Americans.

In 1930, the Cooperative Business Professional and Labor League of Cook County, Chicago, provided a granite monument for Coleman's grave site. At the unveiling ceremony, the Reverend Junius Austin read a letter from the assistant secretary of commerce of the United States: "I trust that this monument will not only serve to commemorate her achievements and sacrifices but also to stimulate others of her race to high purposes and worthy accomplishments."[5]

High purposes and worthy accomplishments were achieved by many of Coleman's followers. African-American Willa Brown, for one, learned to fly at Chicago Aeronautical University in 1930. She then went on to train a large number of African-American flight students in her South Side school. These men went on to become the Tuskegee Airmen, one of the most highly decorated fighter pilot groups in World War II.

In a lecture in Santa Monica, California, Bessie Coleman had once prophesied, "I am anxious to teach some of you to fly, for accidents may happen. I may drift out and there would be someone to take my place."[6] Other African Americans did take her place at lecture podiums and in the skies. African-American lieutenant William J. Powell lived in Chicago during Coleman's exhibition days. In 1929, he established the Bessie Coleman Aero Club and School in Los Angeles. In 1931, at the Los Angeles East Side Airport, the Bessie Coleman Aero Club put on the first all-black public air show. Fifteen thousand spectators attended. Three years later, Powell wrote *Black Wings*, a book he dedicated to the memory of Bessie Coleman. "Because of Bessie Coleman, we have overcome that which was much worse than racial barriers. We have overcome the barriers within ourselves and dared to dream."[7] At

"Because of Bessie Coleman . . . we have overcome the barriers within ourselves and dared to dream," wrote William J. Powell, another early African-American aviator.

that time Powell claimed there were 18,041 pilots in the United States; only twelve were African American. He believed that African Americans would never be free men and women in the South until they could ride in airplanes they themselves owned and operated.

As more African Americans took to the skies, they began forming flight schools and organizations. In 1931, the Challenger Air Pilot Association was founded in Chicago. This national organization of African-American aviators constructed its own airfield in the African-American township of Robins, Illinois, because African American pilots were not permitted to use the Chicago airport. The association started an annual tradition to pay tribute to Bessie Coleman and her inspiring legacy: A group of single-engine planes would fly in formation over her grave. One plane would leave the formation to drop a wreath and rose petals on the grave. As the pilots aged and retired, the custom stopped for a while, but it was revived in the 1980s.

In 1932, James Banning made the first successful transcontinental flight by an African American. Five schools had refused to train him, but like Bessie Coleman he did not give up. He and his mechanic, Thomas C. Allen, called themselves the Flying Hoboes because they had a used plane and no money.

Two other persistent African-American pilots were Tobert Abbott Dale White and Chauncey E. Spencer.

They flew in an old plane to Washington, D.C., to meet with Senator Harry S. Truman. Their purpose was to persuade him to promote Air Force training for African Americans. Truman looked at their plane and said, "If you had guts enough to fly this thing to Washington, I've got guts enough to see that you get what you are asking for."[8]

After pressure from African-American groups, the Air Corps started training the first all-black regiment of airmen in 1941. A full-service base—the Tuskegee Army Air Field—was built for the training of fighter pilots. During World War II, the Tuskegee Airmen carried out more than two hundred missions. Escorting planes to German sites, they never lost a single bomber to enemy fire.

Bessie Coleman's memory lives on in Chicago. In 1977, a group of black women from Chicago and Gary, Indiana, formed the Bessie Coleman Aviators Club. A street beside the Midway Airport was named Bessie Coleman Drive. In 1986, Mayor Richard M. Daley proclaimed April 26 Bessie Coleman Day. In 1993, a $2.6-million library was named after Bessie Coleman, whose dream of becoming a pilot had started with reading books. Her name is also on a section of a hangar at the Aerospace Vocational-Technical Center.

The Federal Aviation Administration paid tribute to Coleman by creating the "Bessie Intersection." Intersections are radio frequencies used by low-flying pilots to identify their location. Pilots flying over a site about forty miles northwest of O'Hare International Airport in Chicago used to say they were at V228 and V420. Pilots can now identify this location as the Bessie Intersection.

In 1986, Marion Coleman, Bessie's niece, started a petition for a commemorative postage stamp in her aunt's honor. With the determination and fortitude of Bessie herself, Marian Coleman followed the project through completion. In May 1995, the thirty-two-cent first-class stamp was issued as part of the Black Heritage series.

Cyrus C. Cassells, Jr., a NASA engineer, honored Bessie Coleman at a ceremony at the San Diego Aerospace Museum in 1995. He told of her part in inspiring and encouraging African Americans to learn to fly. He introduced some distinguished African-American pilots and officers in the audience as examples of Coleman's legacy. "We all shared Bessie's love for flying and went through the door that she cracked open."[9]

Throughout Bessie Coleman's career, she never received as much support and publicity as the white women pilots of her time. Their paths never crossed either by choice or by chance. Sixty years after Coleman's death, she and Amelia Earhart were recognized together in the International Friendship Forest in Atchison, Kansas. The park was created in 1986 as a

Marion Coleman holds a photograph of her famous aunt Bessie.

bicentennial gift to the United States from the International Ninety-Nines, an organization founded by Amelia Earhart. It is planted with trees representing club members all over the world. Next to two of these trees are granite plaques, one engraved with the name Amelia Earhart, the other with Bessie Coleman. Both commemorate "exceptional contributions to aviation."[10]

In the beginning, Coleman did not set out to make a contribution to aviation. She simply wanted to learn to fly. Fearlessly, she strove toward that goal, becoming the first licensed African-American pilot and the first black woman in the world to be a pilot.

Her hard work and determination led to exceptional contributions to aviation and to society. She used her skills and fame to improve the lives of others. She traveled, lectured, and entertained. She demanded equal treatment for everyone in her audiences, regardless of race. Her skillful flying disproved any notions that African Americans and women could not learn to fly a plane. She gave African Americans the opportunity to soar above their cities and farmlands. And she started the movement to create aviation schools to train future African-American pilots.

Just before her death, Coleman spent some time teaching African-American children that they, too, could become aviators.[11] In Orlando she visited public schools and spoke to the students. The afternoon before her accident, Coleman had visited every public school in Jacksonville and talked with the children. Ruby Mae McDuffie—the twelve-year-old girl who wrote the letter found in Coleman's pocket after her death—was only one of the many youngsters inspired by Coleman. Bessie Coleman's success taught her that anything is possible if you don't give up. Ruby Mae could grow up to become a pilot, a doctor, or whatever she set her sights on.

Bessie Coleman's influence reached beyond the field of aviation. She flew loops and stunts in borrowed planes and rickety old Jennies, and her message continues to soar: Don't be afraid to take risks. Fly!

CHRONOLOGY

1892—Bessie Coleman is born on January 26 in Atlanta, Texas.

1895—Coleman family moves to Waxahachie, Texas.

1898—Bessie starts school.

1901—Bessie's father leaves the family.

1903—Coleman works as a laundress; Orville and Wilbur Wright make their first successful flight in an air machine.

1910—Coleman attends Colored Agricultural and Normal University in Langston, Oklahoma, for one year.

1915—Moves to Chicago, Illinois, in search of a better life; enrolls at the Burnham School of Beauty Culture.

1916—Works at the White Sox Barbershop as a manicurist; secretly marries Claude Glenn on December 30.

1920—After being refused flying lessons, Coleman goes to Robert Abbott, owner of the *Chicago Defender*, for advice about how to pursue her dream of learning to fly.

1921—Enrolls in aviation school in France; earns an international pilot's license, becoming the first black woman in the world with a pilot's license; attends the Pan African Congress in Paris; arrives back in New York on September 29.

1922—Returns to France to learn aviation stunt flying; then comes back to the United States to earn money performing in air shows; in Garden City, Long Island, makes the first public flight of an African-American woman pilot, giving African Americans rides in her plane after the show; decides to work toward opening a flight school for African Americans.

1923—Gives lectures and air shows to raise money for a school; purchases a World War I surplus biplane; crashes in Santa Monica, California; sustains a broken leg and other injuries, and her plane is ruined.

1923—Takes some time off from flying.

1925—Returns to Texas; begins exhibitions and lectures throughout the South; purchases another used plane; demands that segregation rules be suspended, allowing blacks and whites to use the same entrance to her show.

1926—On April 30, on a practice flight before an air show in Jacksonville, Florida, Coleman falls from the plane to her death.

Chapter Notes

Chapter 1. Flying with a Purpose

1. Sherwood Harris, *The First to Fly: Aviation's Pioneer Days* (New York: Simon & Schuster, 1970), p. 287.

2. Editorial, *The New York Times*, June 7, 1921, p. 16, cited in Kathleen Brooks-Pazmany, *United States Women in Aviation* (Washington, D.C.: Smithsonian Institution Press, 1991), p. 4.

3. *Houston Post-Dispatch*, June 18, 1925, p. 1.

4. "Flying Circus Unusual Event to Be Repeated," *Houston Informer*, June 27, 1925, p. 1.

Chapter 2. Growing Up Southern

1. Elois Coleman Patterson, *Memoirs of the Late Bessie Coleman, Aviatrix: Pioneer of the Negro People in Aviation* (privately published by Elois Coleman Patterson, 1969), p. 12.

2. August Meier and Elliott Rudwick, *From Plantation to Ghetto* (New York: Hill and Wang, 1976), p. 204.

3. Doris L. Rich, *Queen Bess, Daredevil Aviator* (Washington, D.C.: Smithsonian Institution Press, 1993), p. 6.

4. Ibid., p. 5.

5. "Waxahachie Was a Teeming Hub," Historic Waxahachie Driving Tour Map (Waxahachie, Tex.: Historic Waxahachie, Inc., 1987).

6. Ibid.

7. Patterson, p. 12.

8. Personal interview with Marion Coleman, niece of Bessie Coleman, August 20, 1999.

9. Jacqueline Jones, *Labor of Love, Labor of Sorrow: Black Women, Work and the Family from Slavery to the Present* (New York: Basic Books, 1985), p. 123.

10. Patterson, p. 12.

11. Ibid.

12. Personal interview with Marion Coleman, August 20, 1999.

13. Patterson, p. 13.

14. Rich, p. 9.

15. Paul Laurence Dunbar, *The Complete Poems of Paul Laurence Dunbar, 1940* (New York: Dodd, Mead & Company, 1970).

16. Patterson, p. 12.

17. Ibid.

18. Rich, p. 10.

19. Patterson, p. 13.

20. Archived advertisement, Robert L. Parkinson Library and Research Center, Circus World Museum, Baraboo, Wisconsin.

21. Patterson, p. 13.

22. Rich, p. 14.

23. Ibid., p.13.

24. Elizabeth Amelia Hadley Freydberg, *Bessie Coleman: The Brownskin Lady Bird* (New York: Garland Publishing, 1994), p. 68.

25. Patterson, p. 13.

26. Ibid., p. 14.

27. Frank Marrero, "The Forgotten Father of Aerobatics," *Flight Journal*, April 1999, p. 42.

Chapter 3. Seeking Independence

1. Larry Viskichil, *Chicago at the Turn of the Century in Photographs* (New York: Dover Publications, 1984), p. ix.

2. Travis Dempsey, *An Autobiography of Black Chicago* (Chicago: Urban Research Press, 1981), p. xviii.

3. Elois Coleman Patterson, *Memoirs of the Late Bessie Coleman, Aviatrix: Pioneer of the Negro People in Aviation* (privately published by Elois Coleman Patterson, 1969), p. 14.

4. Ibid.

5. Travis, p. 37.

6. Stanley Dance, *The World of Earl Hines* (New York: De Capo Press, 1977), p. 61.

7. Doris L. Rich, *Queen Bess, Daredevil Aviator* (Washington, D.C.: Smithsonian Institution Press, 1993), p. 23.

8. Arna Bontemps and Jack Conroy, *Anyplace But Here* (New York: Hill and Wang, 1966; originally published as *They Seek a City*, 1945), pp. 175–176.

9. Patterson, p. 2.

10. C. V. Glines, "Airmail's First Day," *Aviation History*, May 1994 <http://www.thehistorynet.com/ AviationHistory/ articles/0594_text.htm> (March 8, 2001).

11. Valerie Moolman, *Women Aloft* (Alexandria, Va.: Time-Life Books, 1981), p. 13.

12. Ibid., p. 33.

13. Patterson, p. 2.

14. Emmett Dedmon, *Fabulous Chicago: A Great City's History and People* (New York: Atheneum, 1981), pp. 288–289.

15. Personal interview with Marion Coleman, August 20, 1999.

16. Dance, p. 61

17. Personal interview with Marion Coleman.

Chapter 4. Passing the Test

1. Valerie Moolman, *Women Aloft* (Alexandria, Va.: Time-Life Books, 1981), p. 18.

2. Kathleen Brooks-Pazmany, *United States Women in Aviation, 1919–1929* (Washington, D.C.: Smithsonian Institution Press, 1991), p. 1.

3. Margery Brown, "What Men Flyers Think of Women Pilots," *Popular Aviation*, March 1929, p. 62.

4. Elois Coleman Patterson, *Memoirs of the Late Bessie Coleman, Aviatrix: Pioneer of the Negro People in Aviation* (privately published by Elois Coleman Patterson, 1969), p. 14.

5. Roi Ottley, *The Lonely Warrior: The Life and Times of Robert Abbott* (Chicago: Henry Regnery Company, 1955), p. 268.

6. Ibid., p. 269.

7. Patterson, p. 5.

8. Elizabeth Amelia Hadley Freydberg, *Bessie Coleman: The Brownskin Lady Bird* (New York: Garland Publishing, 1994), p. 74.

9. Doris L. Rich, *Queen Bess, Daredevil Aviator* (Washington, D.C.: Smithsonian Institution Press, 1993), p. 31.

10. Ibid., p. 32.

11. Patterson, p. 2.

12. John Maxtone-Graham, *Liners to the Sun* (New York: Macmillan Publishing Co., 1985), p. 4.

13. "Exclusive Interview," *Chicago Defender*, October 8, 1921, p. 2.

14. Rich, p. 34.

15. "Exclusive Interview," p. 2.

16. Madeline G. Allison, *The Crisis*, December 1922, pp. 74–75.

17. "Exclusive Interview," p. 2.

18. Ibid.

19. Ibid.

20. "'Shuffle Along' Company Gives Fair Flyer Cup," *Chicago Defender*, October 8, 1921, p. 2.

Chapter 5. Showing Off

1. "Bessie Coleman Leaves New York for France," *Chicago Defender*, February 25, 1922.

2. "Negro Aviatrix Arrives: Bessie Coleman Flew Planes of Many Types in Europe," *The New York Times*, August 14, 1922, p. 4.

3. Ibid.

4. Ibid.

5. Elizabeth Amelia Hadley Freydberg, *Bessie Coleman: The Brownskin Lady Bird* (New York: Garland Publishing, 1994), p. 84.

6. "Negro Aviatrix Arrives," p. 4.

7. Ibid.

8. Doris L. Rich, *Queen Bess, Daredevil Aviator* (Washington, D.C.: Smithsonian Institution Press, 1993), p. 46.

9. "Negro Aviatrix Arrives," p. 4.

10. "World's Greatest Woman Flyer Protégé of the World's Greatest Weekly," *Chicago Defender*, September 2, 1922, p. 3.

11. "Bessie to Fly Over Gotham," *Chicago Defender*, August 25, 1922.

12. "Heart-Thrilling Stunts," *Chicago Defender*, September 2, 1922, p. 3.

13. "Bessie Gets Away; Does Her Stuff," *Chicago Defender*, September 9, 1922, p. 3.

14. *Baltimore Afro-American*, September 15, 1922, p. 9.

15. Elois Coleman Patterson, *Memoirs of the Late Bessie Coleman, Aviatrix: Pioneer of the Negro People in Aviation* (privately published by Elois Coleman Patterson, 1969), p. 5.

Chapter 6. Crashing in California

1. Elois Coleman Patterson, *Memoirs of the Late Bessie Coleman, Aviatrix: Pioneer of the Negro People in Aviation* (privately published by Elois Coleman Patterson, 1969), p. 5.

2. "Bessie Coleman Makes Initial Aerial Flight," *Chicago Defender*, October 21, 1922.

3. Ibid.

4. "Bird Woman Here," *Baltimore Afro-American*, November 10, 1922, p. 3.

5. "Bessie Coleman Breaks Contract," *Baltimore Afro-American*, December 1, 1922, p. 13.

6. "Bird Woman Here," p. 3.

7. Jack R. Lincke, *Jenny Was No Lady* (New York: W. W. Norton & Company, 1970), p. 5.

8. "Bessie Coleman Says Good Will Comes from Hurt," *Chicago Defender*, March 10, 1923.

9. "Aviatrix Falls 300 Feet Here," Santa Monica *Evening Outlook*, February 5, 1923.

10. Ibid.

11. "Flies All Over Europe," *California Eagle*, February 10, 1923, p. 1.

12. "No Flight by Bessie Coleman, Rain Interferes," *Chicago Defender*, September 8, 1923, p. 2.

13. "Bessie Coleman Says Good Will Comes From Hurt."

14. "Other Race Appreciates Girl Flyer," *California Eagle*, March 4, 1923.

15. "Queen Bess Opens School," *The New Age*, May 8, 1923, p. 4.

16. "Bessie Coleman Says Good Will Comes from Hurt."

17. "Bessie Coleman Will Be Seen in Y Movies and in Person," *California Eagle*, April 29, 1923.

18. "Bessie in Booster Role," *Chicago Defender*, June 23, 1923.

Chapter 7. Taking Charge

1. Elizabeth Amelia Hadley Freydberg, *Bessie Coleman: The Brownskin Lady Bird* (New York: Garland Publishing, 1994), p. 90.

2. "Aviatrix to Fly at Driving Park" and "Gigantic Klanvacation: Knights and Ladies of the Ku Klux Klan," *Columbus Dispatch*, September 2, 1923, pp. 2, 38.

3. "No Flight by Bessie Coleman, Rain Interferes," *Chicago Defender*, September 8, 1923, p. 2.

4. Ibid.

5. "Aviatrix Loses Another Manager," *Baltimore Afro-American*, May 2, 1925.

6. *Houston Post-Dispatch*, September 9, 1925, p. 11.

7. Personal interview with Marion Coleman, August 20, 1999.

8. Ibid.

9. Elois Coleman Patterson, *Memoirs of the Late Bessie Coleman, Aviatrix: Pioneer of the Negro People in Aviation* (privately published by Elois Coleman Patterson, 1969), p. 7.

10. Freydberg, p. 91.

11. *Houston Post-Dispatch*, May 7, 1925, p. 4.

12. Patterson, p. 6.

13. Ibid., p. 5.

14. Ibid., p. 7.

15. "'Bird' Woman Falls 2,000 Feet to Death," *Baltimore Afro-American*, May 8, 1926, p. 1.

16. Patterson, p. 6.

17. Ibid., p. 7.

18. Ibid.

19. "Florida Mayor Drinks Toast to 'Brave Bess,'" *Chicago Defender*, May 15, 1926, p. 2.

20. Freydberg, p. 94.

21. Doris L. Rich, *Queen Bess, Daredevil Aviator* (Washington, D.C.: Smithsonian Institution Press, 1993), p. 104.

22. Norman Letters, Black Film Center Archive, Indiana University, Bloomington, February 3, 1926.

23. Rich, p. 103.

24. Patterson, p. 8.

25. "'Bird' Woman Falls 2,000 Feet to Death."

26. Ibid.

Chapter 8. Gambling with Death

1. "Bessie Coleman, Aviatrix, Killed," *Chicago Defender*, May 8, 1926, p. 1.

2. Elois Coleman Patterson, *Memoirs of the Late Bessie Coleman, Aviatrix: Pioneer of the Negro People in Aviation* (privately published by Elois Coleman Patterson, 1969), p. 8.

3. Ibid.

4. E. B. Jourdain, Jr., "Two Lives Snuffed Out When Plane Crashes Down," *Chicago Defender*, May 7, 1926.

5. Ibid.

6. "Bessie Coleman and White Pilot in 2,000-Ft. Crash," *New York Amsterdam News*, May 6, 1926.

7. Patterson, p. 8

8. "Bessie Coleman, Aviatrix, Killed."

9. Patterson, p. 9.

10. Evangeline Roberts, "Chicago Pays Parting Tribute to 'Brave Bessie' Coleman," *Chicago Defender*, May 15, 1926.

11. "Bessie Coleman, Aviatrix, Killed."

12. Alfred B. Smith, *Inspiring Hymns* (Grand Rapids, Mich: Singspiration, 1951), p. 22.

13. Roberts.

14. "Funeral of Aviatrix," *Baltimore Afro-American*, May 15, 1926, p. 1.

15. Roberts.

16. Ibid.

17. Ibid.

18. Ibid.

19. Personal visit to grave site, August 21, 1999.

Chapter 9. Searching for the Truth

1. "Bessie Coleman Fell a Mile," *Baltimore Afro-American*, May 15, 1926, p. 2.

2. Elois Coleman Patterson, *Memoirs of the Late Bessie Coleman, Aviatrix: Pioneer of the Negro People in Aviation* (privately published by Elois Coleman Patterson, 1969), p. 9.

3. Ibid., p. 8.

4. Personal interview with Marion Coleman, August 20, 1999.

5. "Bessie Coleman and White Pilot in 2,000-Ft. Crash," *New York Amsterdam News*, May 6, 1926.

6. Personal interview with Marion Coleman.

Chapter 10. Leading the Way

1. *Norfolk Journal and Guide*, May 15, 1926, p. 14.

2. *Dallas Express*, May 15, 1926, editorial page.

3. Elois Coleman Patterson, *Memoirs of the Late Bessie*

Coleman, Aviatrix: Pioneer of the Negro People in Aviation (privately published by Elois Coleman Patterson, 1969), pp. 9–10.

4. "Harlem's Newest Apartments Named After Black 'Joan of Arc,'" *Chicago Defender*, July 23, 1927.

5. Letter from W. P. MacCracken, Jr., Assistant Secretary of Commerce for Aeronautics, to Oscar C. Brown, Cooperative Business, Professional and Labor League, May 26, 1928. Cited in Elizabeth Amelia Hadley Freydberg, *Bessie Coleman: The Brownskin Lady Bird* (New York: Garland Publishing, 1994), p. 114.

6. "Broken Leg Fails to Daunt Bessie Coleman," *Baltimore Afro-American*, February 23, 1923, p. 12

7. William J. Powell, *Black Aviator: The Story of William J. Powell* (Washington, D.C.: Smithsonian Institution Press, 1994).

8. Freydberg, p. 117.

9. Cyrus Cassells, Jr., speech at the Bessie Coleman Commemorative Stamp Event, San Diego Aerospace Museum, May 11, 1995, and personal conversations.

10. Freydberg, p. 118.

11. Doris L. Rich, *Queen Bess, Daredevil Aviator* (Washington, D.C.: Smithsonian Institution Press, 1993), pp. 103, 108.

FURTHER READING

Borden, Louise. *Fly High! The Story of Bessie Coleman.* New York: Simon & Schuster Publishing, 2001.

Hart, Philip. *Up in the Air: The Story of Bessie Coleman.* Minneapolis, Minn.: Lerner Publications, 1996.

Haskin, James. *Black Eagles: African-Americans in Aviation.* New York: Scholastic, Inc., 1996.

Jones, Stanley. *African-American Aviators.* Mankato, Minn.: Capstone Press, 1998.

INTERNET ADDRESSES

Bessie Coleman: highlights of Coleman's life and career.
<http://www.bessiecoleman.com>

Woman in Aviation Resource Center's Bessie Coleman page.
<http://www.women-in-aviation.com/cgi-bin/ wiarc/links/ detail.cgi?ID=334>

Smithsonian National Air and Space Museum: Coleman's aviation accomplishments.
<http://www.nasm.edu/nasm/aero/women_aviators/ bessie_coleman.htm>

INDEX

Page numbers for photographs are in **boldface** type.